YOUR VISUAL CONNECTION

Your Visual Connection

6 Gesture Types for Holding the 4th Wall

Colum Parke Morgan

COPYRIGHT © 2023 COLUM MORGAN
All rights reserved.

YOUR VISUAL CONNECTION
Six Gesture Types for Holding the Fourth Wall
First Edition

ISBN 978-1-5445-4009-2 *Hardcover*
        978-1-5445-4008-5 *Paperback*
        978-1-5445-4010-8 *Ebook*

*I dedicate this book to three extraordinary mothers:
Kate Shaw-Nappi, MaryBeth
Cavanaugh, and Maura Morgan*

Contents

Introduction   ix

PART I
Chapter 1   A Brief History of the Six Gesture Types   3
Chapter 2   Introducing the Six Gesture Types   19

PART II
Chapter 3   The Body as an Instrument   33
Chapter 4   What the Body Says   49
Chapter 5   Gestures and Reality   83
Chapter 6   Making Our Gestures Matter   103
Chapter 7   Leaning into Character Actions and Interactions   125
Chapter 8   Building Your Practice   147

Conclusion   181
Acknowledgments   185
Appendix   189
Author Bio   199

Introduction

As humans, we're communicative by nature, gossipy at times, and full of stories we like to share. In the midst of so much talking and sharing, rarely do we stop to think about the mechanics of how we communicate: the tone of voice we use at different times; the way we use our eyes to convey meaning; or the role our gestures play in helping to get our points across.

We have all been using gestures and gesture types since we were born. Still, most of us don't realize how important our gestures are when it comes to communicating. The messages our bodies share via posture, hands, and eyes heavily influence the information we convey to audiences—more than that of our voice or the words we use. Knowing and embodying the gesture types, including what they are and what they mean for you, may be your key to commanding the fourth wall and holding your audience's attention.

My own story in relation to the gesture types, the biomechanics of movement, and physical performance started in my teens, when I began to weight train. Biomechanics, anatomy, and the ways that various muscle groups worked together fascinated me then, and still do. I brought this physical awareness into my theatre studies, and eventually into my acting and life as a theatre teacher.

In 2007, after I finished my graduate studies, I worked with a repertory theatre company in California as a resident actor and movement teacher. Strangely enough, my graduate program hadn't delved too deeply into movement or physical theatre, though I had studied both as an undergrad. With my career just getting started, I felt like I was missing a vital understanding of performance. I reached out to an old professor and told her that I wanted to learn more about the body as part of performance. She suggested training in Europe, where I could immerse myself in a deeper understanding of physical acting.

A Physical Acting Education

During my stay in Europe, I was the only American student in an immersive workshop in Italy, where I studied Russian performance methods that emphasized Konstantin Stanislavsky's later theories, Vsevolod Meyerhold, and Michael Chekov. These methods of physical actions and

INTRODUCTION

active analysis were brand-new to me and began to open up a greater understanding of what my body could do as part of physical performance. Before I returned to the States, I traveled throughout parts of eastern Europe, and was amazed that I could enjoy theatre everywhere I went without understanding the languages that actors spoke onstage. They were performing their parts as much with their bodies as with their words.

This first excursion to Europe was brief but poignant. When I returned to the States, I began incorporating various rehearsal techniques I'd studied overseas with great results. I was memorizing roles faster and creating more dynamic, embodied characters. I also found that my comedic timing improved.

Not long after, I took an opportunity to live and work in Europe for a longer period of time. In many ways, this was a new beginning, and an opportunity to expand my understanding of physical performance.

I started my second European journey at L'École Internationale de Théâtre Jacques Lecoq in France, an old boxing gym in the tenth arrondissement of Paris. In his lifetime, Lecoq had encouraged students to explore their physical creativity until they found their own distinct styles. The teachers who ran the school were committed to the same thing. They looked for ways to pull out our creativity so we could find our own answers. Like Lecoq, they didn't want to codify the

YOUR VISUAL CONNECTION

meaning behind a particular skill. Instead, they wanted us to follow our own paths as we improved our performances and discovered what physical imagination meant for us.

Part of the work involved using masks, starting with the neutral mask. Here's an example of the type of neutral mask I worked with.

Alfredo Iriarte, untitled, leather, Mascaras Iriarte, Argentina, *www.mascarasiriarte.com.ar.*

What you see is a symmetrical, nondescript face with soft brows, and a mouth that looks like it's ready to say just about anything, completely free of a single emotion. Working with

INTRODUCTION

the neutral mask was a way for students to feel and respond to the way the world affected their bodies—to understand it both from the outside-in, as well as inside-out, embrace the unknown, and become comfortable in an uncertain space.

What started as ten weeks at the Lecoq school became a five-year period of intensely self-directed study. I turned my attention elsewhere in order to take on as much as I could within the realm of Europe's physical performance culture: studying masks, rhythm, and movement analysis with Norman Taylor, a contemporary of Lecoq; Meyerhold's theatrical biomechanics with Gennady Bogdanov in Italy; the fundamentals of the Michael Chekov technique in Paris; Lessac voice training in Dublin; corporeal miming with Theatre de l'Ange Fou in London. But it was with Thomas Prattki in Berlin where I learned Integral Movement, a new conduit between physical action and subconscious thought. In the process, the idea of physicality and self-expression took on a completely new position in my thinking and being.

Our Bodies Are Content

Did you know that most American theatre and performance education is based on emotional work? Reflecting again on my studies in the States, including a Meisner acting intensive, I'd learned that the body is primarily a device for performing physical and psychological actions. Teachers and practices throughout Europe introduced me to something vastly different from what I'd learned by studying American Realism: the body is built to receive, carry, and convey content.

In the American Realism method, students and performers spend a lot of time analyzing a script, then finding their motivations. They act from that emotional or psychological place, and eventually physicalize the body's response. For example, imagine that, as performers, we want to exhibit fear in a scene. First, we invoke a place where we feel fear—maybe we revisit or imagine a childhood trauma. Then, we give the emotion to the body, and our body takes on the physical appearance of fear.

Even the first teachers of American Realism, like Sanford Meisner or Lee Strasberg, and the various methods that followed them, tended to view the body through the lens of action, not gesture. They focused on the internal or psychological manifestations of actions—an inside-out approach that starts with the actor's body as is and develops the character from there. They addressed physicality later in the process.

In Europe, I was learning an outside-in method that said the body and the gestures can drive the experience toward the emotion and communicate levels of information in exciting ways. Movements can connect us to characters and take us into new emotional spaces. In other words, we can move ourselves into an emotion. For instance, we can vigorously pull on our beard, slowly shift our balance from foot to foot, switch our gaze between two points on the ground, and repeat in a whisper, "I don't remember." We can let gestures transform our actions and create new emotion, thereby altering our performance.

I also learned a number of valuable lessons outside of the classroom, just from living in foreign countries. Moving throughout parts of western and eastern Europe, I was less than fluent in local languages. To make my way around, I relied on gestures to get answers and convey information. From trying to find the market, to figuring out how to grab a cab, everything became an extension of my studies. I was embodying the gestures all day long, whether I was trying to grow as an actor or navigate life. In the process, I started to acquire different languages at levels that seemed to be beyond my intellect, because I was literally incorporating them as I was gesturing for pastries or miming my symptoms at a pharmacy to get the right medicine.

I started to see a similar dynamic play out in classes and performance spaces. Those of us who didn't understand the local languages seemed to take to the physical studies and practices better than native speakers. To actually understand the instructions and the scene without knowing the spoken language required an intense gestural control. We had to push beyond the limitations of verbal speech in order to produce performances that others could enjoy and understand.

Getting the Question, Finding the Answer

I came back to the States in August of 2016, and settled in Austin, Texas, in part to help take care of a family obligation. I began working with local acting students on audition preparation, where one is asked to present two contrasting monologues in less than two minutes. The performances always improved when we defined clear objectives and actions, but I found that a lot of my students when preparing to give dramatic monologues or speak publicly, didn't know what to do with their hands. In fact, many would come right out and ask me, "What should I do with my hands?"

To help them find the answer, I buried myself in the Austin Public Library, pulling out every book I could find, jumping online for more research, then circling back and forth for hours, days on end. I discovered that a lot of people from many disciplines talked about gestures, but I couldn't find one definitive source that put everything together. I kept looking and looking, leaning into what I'd learned in Europe, pairing this piece of information with that, moving out of the theatre section into business, then into science, through the behavior studies, and even into psychology. Some books said X, others said Y. Many books, especially business-focused ones, wanted to codify the language, as if to say, "When you do this with your hands, you get this result," and so forth.

INTRODUCTION

Eventually, I noticed correlations between what I read in the business and science books and what I'd learned overseas. Some books discussed automatic or affect gestures, the subconscious self-touching of our bodies and faces, the types of things that the director of sales may want to avoid in a big meeting. For performers, we actually want to incorporate these gestures into realistic performances, in order to bring characters to life.

Meanwhile, some of the more science-focused texts were looking at things like the biomechanics of gestures, an analysis of motion, by dividing larger movement into smaller parts. Biomechanics were still fresh in my mind from Europe, and here they were again, but with a scientific focus. I knew there was something more to tease out for performers.

As ideas blended in my mind, I began to simplify everything down to what I viewed as key commonalities. In an interesting way, my background in improvisation, and the philosophy of "Yes, and…" helped. Every connection and correlation was an opportunity to mix and match ideas. Eventually, the experience of delving into the gestures at this level led me to build my curriculum around six gesture types, starting with pointing gestures.

Moving On-screen During the Pandemic

In March of 2019, I made my way up to San Francisco as a chance to start anew. The family obligation that brought me back to Austin was settled, and San Francisco, the third-largest theatre city in the country, was calling. Beyond performing, I'd evolved my theatre classes to incorporate aspects of theatre, art, science, illustration, history, and even business. When I submitted different ideas to various schools in the Bay Area, only one school in the East Bay was interested.

My first classes began in January of 2020, just before the start of the COVID-19 lockdowns. Initially I was set to run three in-person classes: movement analysis with neutral masks, a beginning acting course, and improvised rehearsal techniques and character embodiment using biomechanics. Toward the end of my third course, COVID hit, forcing a room full of courageous students to finish their physically immersive class online.

Being a part of a theatre community was helpful at the start of COVID. Productions of every kind shut down, and we all lost audiences. We rallied together as best we could to support one another as we moved theatre performances online. During these early online productions, most performers thought that adapting would be easy. We were actors, after all—how hard could it be? As I watched performances that were meant for stage take place on screen, the gaps in various performance styles became clear. Certain actors adapted better to performing online than others, which led me to wonder if I could create a series of classes to help others do the

INTRODUCTION

same. Was there a new way to answer the question, "What should I do with my hands?"

Not being able to interact with students in physical space, much less see their full bodies, created some perplexing challenges. When you're in a room with people, it's natural to be aware of the surroundings, objects, and our movements throughout the space. Communicating in a Zoom setting is much different. Being on camera creates a frame around your body. To perform in that space, you have to acutely focus on movements—theirs and your own—in entirely new, more detailed ways.

Onstage, performers share space, either with other actors, a prop, the audience, or a combination. We possess context for what's happening around us, and our gestures reflect this. We shift our eyes, lean against a jukebox, and wag our finger to argue with another character's song choice; we extend the room with our eyes, wave beyond the audience to a departing ship, and weep the word "goodbye." With a phone to our ear, we clutch our throat and gasp, "When?" When the detective asks, "Where'd you put the body?", we glance up at the ceiling and smile.

Presenting yourself on camera is a different animal. Our gestures become more finite. When you're isolated on screen, as most of us were during the early days of COVID, the gestures actually become some of the most important communication tools we have, if not the most important.

Exploring New Spaces

With COVID in the mix, and campus shut down, the spatial dynamics I relied on and worked with as a teacher were gone. I lost my ability to help people become more embodied performers. Still, I saw an opportunity that went back to the "hands" question. In that way, the pandemic forced me to become even more focused on addressing the challenge.

For the first round of on-camera classes, I submitted an idea that was even farther left of the dial than my earlier classes. Once again, the school was supportive, and so were students. The class filled up quickly, along with a waiting list. The same thing happened during the next two sessions, as students came from a number of disciplines, not just theatre. The question of "What should I do with my hands?" was the same, but the meaning had changed. Now it was about living our lives on screen.

During a trip back to Austin, I found myself at a casual birthday party, complete with lots of masks and social distancing. I was making small talk with a young CEO of a company that did business in the oil industry. She knew I was a performer and wanted to know my perspective on how things were going. Her business was trying to adapt, and some of her sales team had been experimenting with video for the first time, to correspond with clients. Per the CEO, the people using videos were having more success

INTRODUCTION

connecting with potential clients than people who opted to stick with email and phone calls. When I told her about my classes, she wanted to know if I'd be interested in training some of her teams.

Until then, I had built my classes for theatre people—students, actors, teachers. I had gone so far into theatricalizing various methods, biomechanics, masks, etc., that it hadn't occurred to me that people outside of theatre would find these concepts beneficial or helpful.

After our conversation, I dove back into my notes and reflected on everything I'd learned in and since Europe. The training I delivered was essentially the same as my theatre workshops, and the results couldn't have been better for the business—the company realized an almost immediate uptick in their sales percentage.

Knowing and Using the Six Gesture Types

For hundreds of years, thespians have been specializing in addressing crowds and conveying meaning via performances. Since the advent of movies and TV, most people on camera were actors, journalists, presenters, and politicians. Things began to change around the early 1990s with the advent of reality TV. But today, nearly everyone with a smartphone can share content with thousands of people almost instantly, yet very few people actually have time to take an acting class.

My goal with this book is to help people communicate more clearly, like actors do.

It's rare in today's world to study gestures, and I hope to bring new insight to some very old ideas from the theatre archives, updated with amazing new science. While lots of business books seek to codify gestures like language, nothing classifies gestures for the general public, or for modern actors. Knowing even a little bit about gesture types can benefit anyone in their quotidian lifestyle, whether on camera, at the bank, or addressing a boardroom, courtroom, or auditorium.

Look around. Do you notice the gestures that people make at different times? Do some people seem to be better physical communicators than others? What about you? No matter where you find yourself on the performance spectrum, *Your Visual Connection* helps you delve into the six gesture types in an easy way, so you can gather information in a small amount of time and put the gestures to use.

This book adds a new level of understanding to what you may intuitively know about your body, as well as how you move at different times and for different effects. Rather than codify physical language, my aim is to share what the different gesture types are, so you can explore and discover your own meanings. While the path I've taken goes through the world of theatre and performance, these tools and concepts can help you become a better communicator regardless of your profession. In the end, no matter where or for whom

INTRODUCTION

any of us perform, our jobs are the same: to hold the fourth wall, and to keep our audiences interested and engaged.

The chapters that follow make connections with modern science, and give you practices you can use in the real world. You'll find insight into new ways to command your physical space, and to answer the fundamental question, "What should I do with my hands?" for yourself.

My hope is that you consider *Your Visual Connection* to be a user's manual for your body. To start, Chapter 1 will take us back to Ancient Rome, then bring the narrative forward to our modern day. Having context of the history is a great way to track the evolution of various gesture types, then connect this history to the world we know today.

PART I

CHAPTER 1

A Brief History of the Six Gesture Types

Knowing the six gesture types involves rethinking the body: how it works and moves; why it does what it does at different times; and how we can gain ownership of our movements for effect and impact. The full history of the gestures covers a large sprawl and goes back to a time that predates spoken language as we know it. It's a fascinating history to explore in detail. In the book's appendix, I've listed a number of the books and resources that I turned to, and continue to turn to, for my own study, and I encourage you to peruse them for your own. For the sake of our conversation, I'd like to start a little more recently in Ancient Rome, then track how our understanding of the gesture types moved forward through rhetoric, art, and science into our modern times.

Ancient Rome

Ancient Rome was not a quiet place, and nearly everyone had something to say. Public speaking in this era was more than an art—it was a central part of what it meant to be a citizen. Roman aristocrats and orators learned public speaking and oratory skills so they could take part in debates and voice their opinions in ways that rose above the clatter. Everyone was talking, competing for attention, and vying to capture and hold the imaginations of their audiences. The best speakers of the time knew that their words alone were not enough. They needed to bring something else—their gestures—into communication. They used them in support of their rhetorical arguments, to aid their deliveries, and to help their audiences follow the emotional and logical thoughts of their argument.

Two names rise up from this era when we consider the gesture types: Marcus Tullius Cicero, and Marcus Fabius Quintilianus (known today as Quintilian). They were

A BRIEF HISTORY OF THE SIX GESTURE TYPES

scholars and teachers, and they created systems of rhetoric that emphasized the role of speaking and oration in society.

As Quintilian and Cicero laid out their specifics within presentation styles, they also codified meanings behind the gestures they prescribed. Effectively, they were saying to their students, "Do these things at different times during your speech: stand this way; let the shoulder of your toga fall at this moment; place the middle finger against the thumb and extend the remaining three," etc. The following page shows an example of different rhetorical hand positions.[1]

They had no interest in teaching everyday gestures and saw a very clear distinction between gestures for oration, which adapt to the emotional and logical content of the entire thought, and those for theatre, such as the gestures involved in mimicry, descriptive action, or pantomime—topics we'll explore throughout this book. Their treatises focused on various rhetorical methods and passed along their codified meanings. Quintilian, who wrote twelve books on the art of rhetoric, dedicated only a portion of his eleventh book to what should happen after a person has written a speech. Sadly for civilization, their influence on gestures waned during the Middle Ages. Certain elements of their treatises remained, but the core messages were muted for a thousand years.

---

1   John Bulwer, *Chirologia: Or, the Natural Language of the Hand* (London: The Harper, 1644), 189.

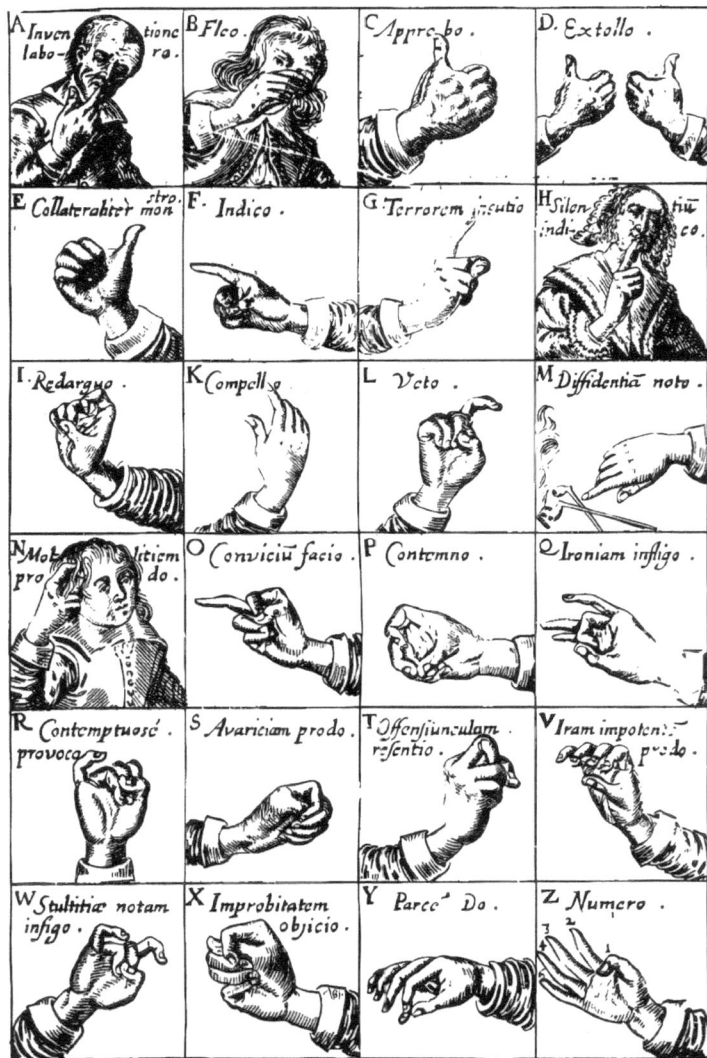

John Bulwer, *Alphabet of Natural Gestures of the Fingers*, 1644, illustration, *Chirologia: Or, the Natural Language of the Hand.*

Theatre and Performance of the Same Era

The earliest group rituals developed into religious ceremonies and involved a great deal of dancing and singing—movements that eventually led to the performance arts, including opera, ballet, and theatre. Discussing the origin of gestures in early theatre quickly takes us to mime and pantomime. Livius Andronicus is credited with having invented pantomime in the year 240 BC, after he lost his voice. In order to continue performing, Andronicus gave a child his lines to speak, while he mimed various parts of the story. This took theatre in a brand-new direction, and audiences found it more exciting than what they were used to—it was as if his body was speaking the words. In the process, Andronicus created a new way to embody separate characters at different times and take on multiple roles in a performance—a true chameleon.

The main difference between orators and performers was that rhetoricians of the time weren't playing characters, but actors were. For that reason, actors who embodied the gestures put more emphasis on playing their masks (stock characters), whereas rhetoricians wanted to appear authentic and genuine, because too much emotion would actually work against an orator—if a senator's face was too expressive, it would come off as being fake, and the people he was trying to sway wouldn't trust him.

- Many of the ideas that Quintilian and Cicero stressed relate to our modern understanding of charisma: controlling the body and emotions; avoiding the use of everyday or affect gesture types (which I'll introduce in Chapter 2 and come back to in Chapter 5); and relaxing the gestures via rhythms.

- Concerning society's earliest actors, we can see them as having focused on embodying characters and approaching the status of chameleons: they brought gestures forward from real life in order to mime words, develop characters with the help of masks, and prompt reactions based on the speed and size of the gestures they made.

Similar to what happened with the works of Cicero and Quintilian on the rhetorical side, society's understanding of gestures related to performance also dimmed during the Middle Ages. To a large degree, leaders in the early Christian church did not approve of many of the comedic gestures that developed in early Roman theatre—they saw them as being obscene or vulgar. Still, the gestures did not disappear during this era. Some found their way into the pomp of various religious ceremonies. As the influence of Christianity grew, priests and preachers used gestures in ways that seemed to have grown straight out of Cicero and Quintilian's influence.

A BRIEF HISTORY OF THE SIX GESTURE TYPES

Coming Back to the Gesture Types

Once Quintilian's work was unearthed in 1416, and then Cicero's a century later, society slowly began to reengage with the gesture types. Still, it took another two hundred years before this knowledge reached broader audiences. The printing press had a lot to do with resurrecting the gestures as a subject of artistic, expressionistic, and eventually scientific study.

Many societal gestures began showing up in paintings: hand positions; a certain crossing of the arms; a tilt of the head; etc. This return of the gestures was often associated with background, class, or the amount of education a person had received. As a sign of societal status, the gestures presented themselves in a number of ways, including as public speech devices, refined actions, and certain postures adorned with vestments and clothing.

By now, the world was entering a new era of exploration and scientific inquiry—the Age of Enlightenment. People were questioning things as never before, explorers were crossing oceans, and colonization was happening throughout the globe. It was a confluence of cultures, ideas, and languages, and some people began to wonder if the gestures represented the root of human communication. Could there exist a universal language prior to spoken words?

As this type of thinking spread, the gestures landed under a new scope of scientific rigor. Academics and social scientists of the era began exploring the gestures through a number of different lenses, including linguistics and anthropology. While Cicero and Quintilian had dealt with the link between gesture and delivery, these new fields were more interested in the foundational origin of language and human expression. They were trying to establish a link across all communications and believed the gestures could take them to the beginning.

On the performance side, the gestures never truly disappeared—at least not yet. One facet I'll delve into later in the book is the fact that the study and understanding of gesture types only started to disappear from theatre in the early part of the twentieth century. Throughout the Middle Ages, small wandering companies of trained actors persisted throughout Europe. By Shakespeare's time, theatre's evolution had more to do with the changing roles of actors than anything else. Stock characters melted into playwriting, and writers began to feature characters based on social classes. Onstage, performers and actors became more and more adept at imitating class behavior, and augmenting the gestures of royalty, servants, thieves, members of the working class, and many others for theatrical effects. Running parallel to this, other Renaissance-era performance types, such as opera and ballet, continued to refine gesture use in their unique performance realms. Painters of the time also incorporated gestures into their work, which had a looping effect: painters used actors to

A BRIEF HISTORY OF THE SIX GESTURE TYPES

pose; people imitated the gestures they saw in art; actors imitated the gestures they saw in the public for effect, and so forth.

With the gestures on display in theatre, dance, art, and ceremonies, society at large took notice of the divide between gesture types and social status. Working or peasant classes tended to use quicker, bawdier gestures that emanated from the lower half of their bodies, whereas upper class or nobility operated with slower, loftier gestures, generally via the upper parts of their bodies—waves, doffs, plus the occasional bow which involved the upper half dipping in salute.

Later in the nineteenth century, François Delsarte, a French singer, orator, and performance teacher credited with creating the first complete system of expression, became the dominant name in the world of gestures and performance. He developed what became known as the Delsarte method, which was meant to help interpret emotional expression in musical and dramatic texts. We'll discuss Delsarte's method in Chapter 4. For now, it's worth noting that the Delsarte method fell out of style once realism and the Stanislavski method took hold of acting and theatrical performance in the early 1920s.

From Linguistics to the Subconscious

Following World War II, language and gestures were mostly studied separately, partially on account of Noam Chomsky's influence. Chomsky proposed in the study of linguistics a notion that suggested we can trace the origin of language back to the subconscious, pulling focus away from observable speech acts, like gestures. A lot of science that followed shifted in this direction.

Albert Mehrabian also comes into the conversation around this time. Mehrabian developed what is known as the "7-38-55 percent rule." In fairness, this is an often misinterpreted outcome of a series of communications he and colleagues embarked upon in the mid-1960s. It's easy to fixate on the numbers, but in the end they are less important than the main takeaways: what we say, and how we say it, is about much more than the words, and a great deal of what we're trying to say comes across nonverbally. Mehrabian and his colleagues were able to study verbal and nonverbal communication at such a granular level thanks to new audiovisual technology—they were among the first group of researchers with the ability to film people in conversation, then play back the conversations and watch what their bodies were doing. Other researchers would continue to do the same.

About a decade after Mehrabian, Desmond Morris published *Manwatching*, one of the first books in decades that focused on gestures. Morris's work helped reinforce Mehrabian's study. No matter what your opinion is of the study, Mehrabian helped to clarify the fact that there was much more happening underneath the surface of our words, via our body language and use of gestures. Mehrabian's work, along with Morris's, and the work of many others that followed, turned society's understanding of what we see and what we hear in a new direction. Spoken words have a role to play, and certainly have their own type of power, but so does the body, especially when our gestures build with the words we speak. More than two millennia after Cicero and Quintilian, the gestures had gone from rhetorical delivery, to being tools that helped distinguish social class and wealth, to being studied under scientific observation.

From Ancient Rome to Today

The modern goals of studying gestures aim at figuring out what came first: thought, gesture, or speech, and whether or not certain signs are universal. Two names to bring into the conversation here are David McNeill and Adam Kendon. Both are instrumental in studying the visible body actions that occur during the activity of speaking: examining the units and phrases of gestures; the use of gesture space; and tracking the way gestures and language interrelate.

Through their work, we begin to see how gestures provide a window into a speaker's mind, and better understand the collaborative relationship between gestures and speech—concepts that helped set the stage for where we've gotten in the twenty-first century.

These modern studies are fueled in part by Kendon's observation[2] that gestures are composed of either two (in/out, up/down) or three movement phases (preparation/stroke/retraction):

- The preparation moves the hand from its rest position into the gesture space.
- The action of the gesture occurs in the stroke, where the meaning of the gesture aligns with its verbal counterpart.
- During retraction, the hand completes the gesture by retracting to a resting position.

Although various "holds" can occur throughout these phases, most gestures follow this three-phase pattern. Today's researchers want to know as much about the preparation of a gesture as possible. Does a person actually see an image in their head first, since they gesture a microsecond before they speak? Here's one reason why this is key: most of us have a few hundred words at our disposal in a split second of thought. However, the gestures give us a visual-spatial system with which to convey what we're thinking. This becomes pretty handy when words fail us. This thought opens the

---

2 Adam Kendon, *Gesture: Visible Action as Utterance* (Cambridge, Cambridge University Press, 2004), 111, Kindle.

A BRIEF HISTORY OF THE SIX GESTURE TYPES

door to looking at gestures as more than just random gesticulations, but as part of a subconscious act that goes along with utterances or verbalization.

Cicero and Quintilian may have been focused on codifying meaning for rhetoricians, but they understood the importance of delivering gestures on a number of levels. As I mentioned in the introduction, very few people on the performance side are talking about gestures today, yet they represent some of the best assets actors can have in their toolkits. Looking at things from a broader perspective, actors, performers, politicians, teachers—nearly everyone—can learn something from taking a closer look at their gestures.

Whether you were an actor or a politician in Ancient Rome, the point of gesturing was to keep people's attention—to control the fourth wall. The same is true today. We all want to stand up, own our space, and keep eyes on us. On the senate floor of Ancient Rome, per Quintilian's instructions, your toga would fall off your left shoulder at the right moment of your speech, and it pointed to a big moment in the midst of your rhetoric.

Even though Cicero and Quintilian were adamant about not being actors, these were people-centered moments. Rhetoricians were working with a rhythm and building toward climactic moments in their speeches as a way to draw people in, hold them at bay, and then give them the rhetorical payoff. We may not see this among modern politicians, who tend to stand behind podiums when they speak or debate, but you certainly see inklings of this in courtrooms, where lawyers lean into their gestures at different times as they try to sway a jury. Now, to make this more consistent with what was happening in Ancient Rome, imagine a lawyer having to get the attention of a room full of people in a train station where everyone talks at once.

What Cicero and Quintilian put into practice was the idea that specific gestures, delivered at key moments, enhanced the quality of a rhetorician's delivery. It helped people understand the message a speaker was trying to convey. Today, new sets of inquiry and interest continue to spring up, from the neurological to the biomechanical.

With so much history to lean into, none of us need to reinvent the great wheel of gesture types. And, with modern science reinforcing the wheel, plus with so many ways to record, study, and share our movements, we have everything we need to refine and master our gestures and expressions in the most finite ways imaginable.

But here's the rub about all this technology at our disposal: we have access to audiences like never before. Every smartphone provides an invitation to share a .gif, video, clip, live feed, or Instagram story without a second thought. With so many fourth walls, we have come all the way back around to the time of Cicero and Quintilian—we're surrounded by noise at every turn, always tuned in, scrolling, and fighting

A BRIEF HISTORY OF THE SIX GESTURE TYPES

our way to catch and keep the attention of others. In many ways, the gestures we use, and how we use them, are the things that make the difference.

The Roman senator's job was to plead for things and ask to be heard. With help from the teachings of Cicero and Quintilian, they used their bodies to grab attention and convey their messages. At the same time, onstage, actors gestured to create character. Thousands of years later, with the advent of silent film, those gestures carried over to the screen. Then, through the spread of realism, performance gestures became small and disappeared into spontaneity. Up until the early 1990s, the importance of using gestures remained in the sphere of only a few groups of people: performers, news anchors, and modern politicians are three that come readily to mind.

Now, with the hundreds of thousands of live streams and the steady blitz of social media content, we're in an era where more people than ever are communicating via screens. That includes you, even if your audience is relegated to a few people in a video conference. Whether you're standing in a room full of people or boxed in by the glowing dot on your phone or computer, you have a message to convey.

Studying and knowing the six gestures connects art and science. Performers have been practicing the six gesture types for hundreds of years. In the last half-century, modern science has finally caught up to the dynamics of these same theatrical tools. When you know the gestures, you have a ticket to stronger, more embodied communications, no matter what room or space you're in. They provide a complete picture of what you're trying to say, and what others are thinking around you.

To take our next step toward putting the gestures to work, I'd like to introduce the six gesture types, and set the stage for our deeper exploration into each.

CHAPTER 2

Introducing the Six Gesture Types

Despite all the chaos of human communication, it's refreshing to think that we can distill the vast majority of our movements down to six gesture types. Chapter 2 provides a brief introduction of the six gesture types that I'll focus on throughout the rest of the book: deictic, iconic, metaphorical, emblematic, affect, and beats. We'll explore each in greater detail in the chapters that follow. By the end of this chapter, you will have gained a new vocabulary around these six gesture types.

More importantly, this chapter begins to reinforce a core element of this book: that learning the gesture types isn't the same as learning to play an instrument for the first time. Your body is the instrument. You've been tuning and playing it your entire life, since you first opened your eyes, which is where we'll begin our introduction of the six gesture types.

Deictic Gestures

Deictic gestures bring things to life. The word "deictic" comes from the Greek root *deiktikos*, which translates to "serving to show or point out." When we use them, we are essentially pointing in order to grab or direct someone else's attention toward something, or in the direction in which we are looking or pointing. We routinely point for placement ("Put the cup over there") or place things in a space ("What's that behind you?"). Just looking in a different direction or establishing a direction in which we want someone else to look are examples of deictic gestures. This is important to note, because even though we scan the features of a person's face, we concentrate mostly on their eyes and mouth.[3]

Imagine an actor who's reading from offstage cue cards. In the middle of saying a line, they look past their partner to the card. In the audience, we see a break in the performance. It may be a small eye point, but it reads large.

---

3   Alfred L. Yarbus, *Eye Movements and Vision*, 1967, translated by Basil Haigh (New York, Plenum Press, 1967), 191

INTRODUCING THE SIX GESTURE TYPES

- Deictic gestures are pretty simple movements. They are the very first gestures that babies make with their eyes, before they have the muscle control to point at something.
- When you make a deictic gesture, you're sending your audience's attention somewhere else: from one noun or thing to another.

There are a number of ways a glance, point, or pivot can work to draw the attention of your audience. When you do, you effectively open the space of the performance. Actors use deictics to create (or divide) a space, by placing things offstage, or beyond the four walls surrounding the audience. For instance:

- Glancing beyond the audience, and waving good-bye to someone or something.
- Talking to a character who's off-screen or offstage, by looking in that direction.
- Glancing to the left or right after you've said something, whether to amplify a joke or create a pause in the rhythm.
- Lastly, deictic gestures gain more emphasis and meaning the more you use them, specifically when you repeat sending or using them as placements, spots, or anchors in space. We'll look at them in greater detail starting in Chapter 3.

Iconic Gestures

Iconic gestures relate to mimicking the physical or concrete world around us. They indicate what's happening around you, explain what an object does, or provide the representation or outline of an object, person, animal, etc. An iconic gesture occurs in three phases, with a preparation, a clear stroke, and a retraction. They tend to be co-speech gestures, meaning they synchronize with the meaning of your words. Iconic gestures also have a relationship to the semantic content of spoken words, coupled with bodily movements, to create people or things in space. For instance:

- You set an unopened jar of peanut butter in front of your friend, make a twisting motion with your hands, and ask, "Can you open this jar? It's stuck." You're imitating the iconic motion or movement of the action ("opening") and the thing ("jar").

- You're searching the kitchen junk drawer, then turn to your housemate and say, "Have you seen the scissors?" while making a scissoring motion with your fingers. They respond, "The big or small scissors?" while referencing the size of the scissors between their thumb and forefinger.

- You're retelling old family stories and you playfully mimic your uncle: 'Yeah…but it was already broken!" simultaneously imitating his posture and a familiar gesture he makes.

In these examples, the content exists (jar, scissors, uncle), and is happening in the real world (the jar is actually stuck). This is a key element for iconic gestures, and differentiates them from metaphoric gestures, which focus on abstractions (more on this below).

In performance, iconic gestures are abundant in mime and pantomime, both of which involve learning how to mimic people and objects in space. We'll discuss iconic gestures in greater detail in Chapter 4.

Metaphoric Gestures

Metaphoric gestures can structure the shape of your argument, and present concepts and ideas as entities (or containers) that exist in physical space. More than anything, they express abstractions (feelings, emotions, etc.) that do not exist in physical (concrete) form. Metaphoric gestures also occur in three phases, with a preparation, stroke, and retraction.

- "She's driving me out of my mind." (The gesture: fingers splayed, vibrating next to your head.)

- "What's your opinion on this?" (The gesture: draw a horizontal circle with your hand.)
- "Let's start with introductions." (The gesture: draw an inward spiral with your finger.)
- "Your words are like music to my ears." (The gesture: celebratory arms opening wide, so as to convey joy or relief.)
- "That's enough for now!" (The gesture: hands tamping down to decrease or minimize.) Or "Let's return to this after lunch." (The gesture: From the chest, pushing an imaginary container to the side to suggest moving an idea physically away from the center.)

Some metaphoric gestures relate to the way we stand or sit, our posture when we walk into a room, or how we establish authority or believability ("proud," "exhausted," "calm," etc.). Like iconic gestures, metaphoric gestures tend to be co-speech. In fact, the majority of all narrative gestures are metaphoric. We'll discuss metaphoric gestures in Chapter 4, as part of the conversation on mime and pantomime.

Emblematic Gestures

Emblematic gestures are usually well-known within a given culture: they're easy to replicate, and we know their meaning without needing words. In fact, emblematic gestures often stand in for words/phrases. For example, consider the message behind what's known as the "hook 'em horns."

- In the U.S., especially in Austin, Texas, the gesture is a rallying cry. If you're a fan of the Texas Longhorn football program, then you've probably seen fans flash this gesture during games.

- Conversely, if you use the same gesture in Italy, you might have some explaining to do. Over there, the same gesture is known as the cuckold gesture, and to use it is the same as calling someone *cornuto*, a cuckold. You can trace this symbol's origin back to early Christianity, which often depicted the devil as having horns.

Of all the gesture types, emblems have the cleanest three-phase structure (prep/stroke/retraction) and we'll discuss them first in Chapter 4, then in greater detail in Chapter 5, in the conversation about realism.

Affect Gestures

Affect gestures typically represent self-touch, or auto-contact gestures: the things we do when we're feeling self-conscious, or uncomfortable. Think of affect gestures as the types of non-speech gestures that we are always performing, often when we're alone, whether we're aware of them or not. For example:

- Scratching our faces while we're talking to someone.
- Quickly itching a body part, or continually dabbing a nose with a tissue.
- Unconsciously playing with a piece of jewelry (necklace or ring) or a piece of clothing (cuff or shirt collar).

If you're a politician, a newscaster, or someone giving an important presentation, you most likely want to cut down on affect gestures as much as possible, to the point of removing them from your physical vocabulary altogether. For actors, however, bringing affect gestures into a performance can help to create an extremely realistic character. We'll discuss affect gestures in Chapter 5.

Beats

Beats make up a majority of our co-speech gestures. We recognize them most from watching political debates, or when someone else is presenting a public talk.

- The beat falls directly on a syllable; we strike beats with our hands while we're speaking in order to emphasize all the important words.

INTRODUCING THE SIX GESTURE TYPES

- One way in which beats stand out is that they only have two phases (preparation and retraction).
- Because there is no stroke phase, the hand rarely changes its shape during the gesture.

Used mostly with the hands, beats also occur in the body. I'll discuss beats at different times throughout the book, and we'll explore them in detail in Chapter 6.

Our Spatial Understanding of the World

I'd like to end Chapter 2 by briefly discussing the spatial relationship that exists between our bodies and our gestures. I'll come back to this topic throughout the book, especially as we delve deeper into specific gesture types.

We discover the world through our bodies. In fact, our understanding of the world is spatially oriented almost from the start. As we're beginning to walk, we learn that "up equals good, down equals bad"; we "run away" from harm, and "run toward" safety; with the same hand, we wave hello in one moment, and tell someone to back off in the next, with just a slight adjustment of the gesture.

When you are speaking with someone, the communication and the connection you create is a gift, or a game to develop and unpack. When I'm talking to you, or you're talking to me, what we're exchanging is more than simply information, gossip, or pleasantries. We're building a connection. When we talk with the gestures, or through the gestures, we're giving each other new ways to understand what we're trying to say. When the gestures align with our speech, it creates a spatial dimension to our verbal content. We're exchanging visual information that accompanies our ideas, concepts, and narratives.

When you incorporate the six gesture types into the way you communicate, it helps others understand what you are saying on a whole-body level, amplifying the gift of connection.

Consider the idea of holding the fourth wall, which is at the heart of this book. The fourth wall is a conceptual barrier, or border, between the people delivering or presenting and those who are receiving or watching it. The term comes from theatre, where it refers to the imaginary wall at the front of the stage that separates the audience from the performers. The audience can see through the wall. Technically, the actors can see beyond the fourth wall as well, but their characters usually cannot. Even if we're in front of a camera, or on a video call, the fourth wall is the camera—the direction toward which you present your ideas to the world.

The purpose of any node of knowledge is to simplify a mystery. For many of us, the way our bodies move at a given moment or time is a mystery, even though we occupy our bodies every hour of the day. Whether we're giving a board

INTRODUCING THE SIX GESTURE TYPES

presentation, toasting a couple at their wedding, or standing up to share something at a school board meeting, we often don't know what to do with our hands. In the second part of the book, we'll go deeper into demystifying the body as we delve into the six gestures and discuss ways to put them to work for us.

PART II

CHAPTER 3

The Body as an Instrument

Babies are masters of deictic gestures. The very first gestures we make are deictic—the whole world is happening in our eyes before we develop the muscle control we need to directly engage with it. Before any of us can speak, or even point, we look at what we want. Then we look beyond what we want and find something new. Eventually, our first hand movements reach up toward the closest adult—we want to be picked up. Soon, we're pointing in the direction where we want someone to carry us. We don't know what anything means—only that when we do X, Y, or Z, something happens.

This is the origin of the deictic gestures: looking up, pointing out, and expanding the world.

Knowing the deictic gestures is the first step in recognizing what creates and holds attention. In this chapter we'll explore the deictic gestures at the biomechanical level through puppetry, with a look at the following:

- How our joints are made to move.
- The importance of where we're looking, and when.
- How we actually deliver deictic gestures, and the speed at which we deliver them.

When Eyes Come to Life

The deictic gestures are all about where you send your attention, and usually involve pointing out or looking toward people or objects, whether or not they exist at the other end of your stare. These gestures are probably very familiar to you. We see them and use them all the time in real life and non-performance situations:[4]

- Pointing or nodding with your eyes to indicate or suggest something else is going on "right over there."

---

[4] Carlo Blasis, *Studi Sulle Arti Imitatrici* (Milan: Tipografia E Libreria Di Giuseppe Chiusi, 1844), 97.

THE BODY AS AN INSTRUMENT

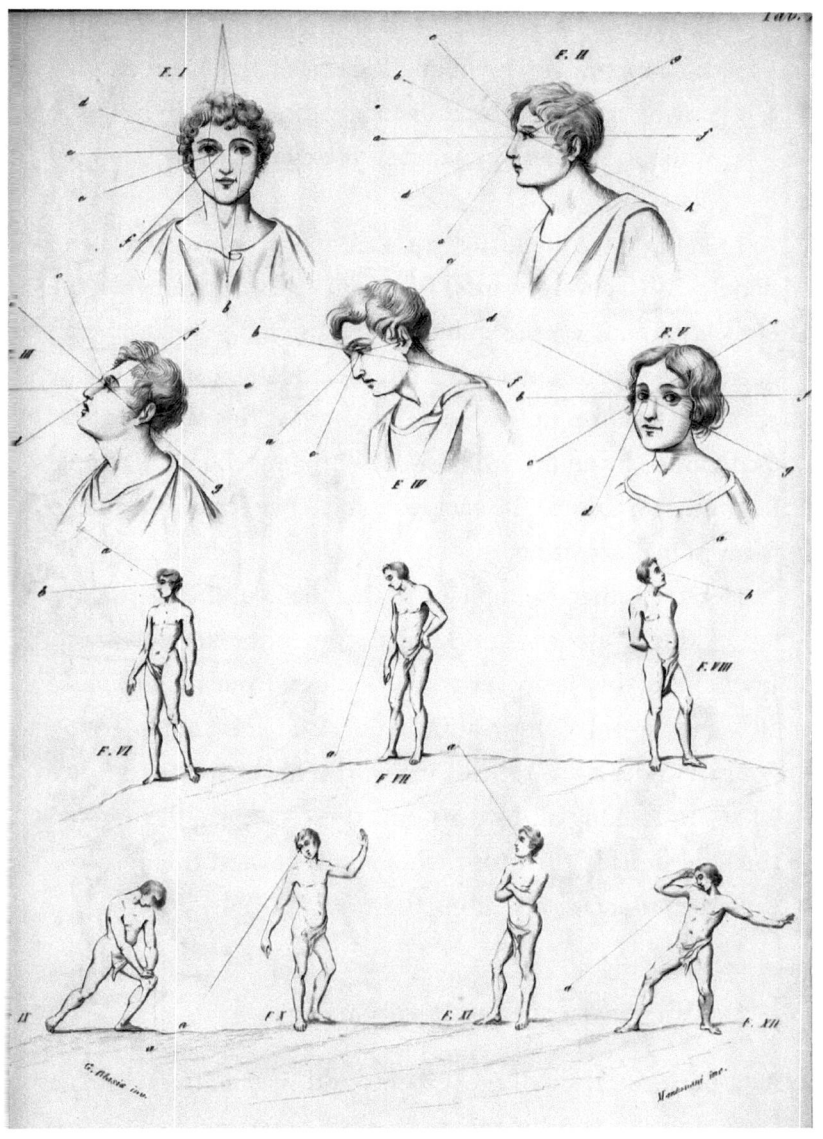

- Using your eyes, hands, and even your entire body in the moment you pivot and look in this new direction.
- Staring beyond your audience and expanding the space of the room just by changing your gaze.

Imagine a street cluster, for a moment, where a circle of people, all facing inwards, focus on something inside the circle (perhaps a cute baby, or a musician). Suddenly, an accident happens outside the circle, and the cluster reacts by shifting attention in this new direction. A few seconds later, as if guided by an inward body-pointing mechanism, people begin to run toward the accident, and a new crowd begins to form in that direction.

Here's another example of deictics in real life. You and I are talking at a party, and I notice someone I know is standing behind you, just over your shoulder. Even though we're still having our conversation, you catch me glancing over your shoulder a few times. Finally, you turn your head to see what I'm looking at. It turns out, you recognize this person too, and quickly turn your whole body toward them, throwing up your arms and calling their name.

Deictic Gestures and Performance

As a performer, small movements and moments can create huge impacts and help you establish brand-new spaces, or anchors within your existing space. When you point toward something with a deictic gesture, you shift your audience's attention in that direction. If we're watching you, we're inclined to want to know what's happening, or what's over there; we believe that the space has opened up behind us, or off the stage or screen.

- The comedian is calmly conversing onstage, then looks out left and yells for his kids to stop jumping off the garage. Then he calmly turns back and continues his conversation. We never actually see any children or a garage in the comedian's bit, but we believe what he's saying, because of where he places his gaze. We're caught in the magic of the gesture, and the idea holds our attention now.

- A character waves at a boat that's sailing away behind our heads; she opens up a brand-new space and extends the world of her performance. Then, she glances at something else a little closer, but still over our heads, or just offstage, and we suspend disbelief once more.

- Takes are another type of deictic that many of us are familiar with, both in performance and real life. A performer may do a double or triple take for a certain effect; or they may do a quick take, or even a slow take (called a slow burn). During his *Saturday Night Live* Weekend Update days, the comedian Norm MacDonald was a master of the off camera take in-between jokes. Another example is the character of Sophia from *Golden Girls*, who delivered many of her lines out, rather than looking directly at the other characters.

If you've auditioned, then you're familiar with how important the deictic gestures can be when you're trying to expand the universe of a room. In an environment where it's just you, a director, and a script, your eyes can go to work as you look off, out, and beyond the walls around you in order to transform the space into a new reality. This is a different approach than acting purely on emotion: you're literally bringing the world into your audition.

Another way to use deictic gestures is to send your attention toward different people at certain times, a tactic that some performers adopt when they're giving a dramatic monologue. This helps you establish anchors in your space—people and areas of the room you'll return to at different times in order to reaffirm their presence and your commitment to the content, subject matter, or performance. A professor in a lecture hall, a parent at a school board meeting, or a salesperson in a corporate meeting could very well do the same thing.

One way to use anchors is by repeating eye points at specific placements in space. Doing so gives special attention to that particular placement. For example, an actor performing a monologue may use two or three anchors to help set people or parts of the room as the proverbial fourth wall. The audience sees the actor set and return to these anchors and starts to associate the anchors as existing within or as part of the actor's performance space. Conversely, a public speaker may use an entirely opposite technique, and choose to sweep over the audience in large arcs, so as to include everyone.

Deictic Gestures in Real Life

Overall, deictic gestures are pretty simple movements. As I wrote at the start of the chapter, they're the very first gestures that babies make with their eyes, before they even have the muscle control to point at something. Eventually, the baby sees her mother, reaches up and babbles, "Mama." We do similar things as adults: visually looking for an object, then at the object, then reaching for it.

"Pointing is, in fact, a specialty of our species," Desmond Morris writes, "and we perform it in many different ways."[5] As humans, we often point things out unintentionally: a quick

---

5 Desmond Morris, *Manwatching. A Field Guide to Human Behaviour*. (London, Jonathan Cape, 1977), 64.

drop of the eyes to someone's shoes, or a return of the head from looking toward a siren. However, if you and I are in a room together, and I point to the window and say, "Hey, look at that amazing bird out there," I've specifically tried to redirect your attention. That is the intent behind my deictic gesture.

This example aligns with David McNeill's research, which suggests that one function of pointing is to make note or bring attention to something that exists in the real world.[6] Wherever we're pointing is essentially a "palpable space," and the object that exists within that space is just that: an object. You probably wouldn't say to your friend who is in the room with you, "Hey, look at that great idea out the window."

But let's stay with that notion for a moment, because McNeill also writes that when you explore the ins and outs of adult conversation, most of our pointing actually does align with abstractions. We point all over the place when we're talking, and these abstract deictics help to create new references in the space we're occupying.[7] We place things in space even when the thing is not in that space. For instance, "that school is too far away," pointing straight at the wall, or "did you lock the garage?" pointing over your shoulder with your thumb.

---

6   David McNeill, *Hand and Mind: What Gestures Reveal about Thought* (Chicago, University of Chicago Press, 1992), 18.
7   David McNeill, *Gesture and Thought*, (Chicago, University of Chicago Press, 2007), 40.

Here's one fascinating aspect of deictic gestures that pairs with performance and real life: they gain more emphasis and meaning the more you use them, specifically when you repeatedly send or use them as placements, spots, or anchors in space. Doing so again and again will direct the attention of others back to the same area.

Puppetry and Biomechanics

Having started with the eyes, let's move into the body with the help of puppetry as a way to understand our body mechanics by using deictic gestures. Before we begin, you don't need to own or borrow a puppet for this section. Just imagine a hand puppet for a moment. It most likely has a torso, a head, maybe even arms connected to long wooden dowels. The head will most likely have eyes of some sort, whether they are stitched in, glued on, or are part of the rubber or plastic molding. Overall, the puppet is probably animated by only a few moving parts.

This hand puppet is fairly anthropomorphic, a stand-in for our own body. As soon as you place it over your hand, you can "bring it to life" by making it look at you, then at a spot on the floor, then back at you, then back to the floor again. These looks are examples of deictic gestures. Maybe you make the puppet turn its head toward you while it slowly drops its mouth. From there you might run the puppet through a sequence of simple movements (touching the forehead or chest, tilting the head while looking at something in the distance, clapping hands together, etc.). These actions aren't deictic gestures, but having started with the simple deictic gesture of looking around, your audience continues to suspend disbelief and sink deeper into the performance.

You can think of these as movements that we make in our own bodies, but simplified. We start by looking at the joints: a body's innate flexibility, and the relationship that exists between various parts and regions of the body. Considering the actions from the above paragraph, the puppet is only as capable as its body allows. The arms are floppy pieces of fabric you can bend to suggest joints. My point is not to turn you into a puppeteer, but to create a window through which we can explore the biometrics of movements through the way the puppet is made and how it moves.

Working with a puppet is a great way to externalize the body and get a sense of looking at it from the outside. But what about working with our own bodies?

Our Bodies and Biomechanics

Let's continue our discussion of biomechanics by looking at the joints of our own bodies, which exist at the center of movement. To start, we'll do a couple of simple exercises to help illustrate the idea and gain a new understanding of how we move at different times, and in different ways. We'll begin with our hands:

- With one hand extended, move your fingers, one at a time. Fan your fingers out. Clench them into a fist. Extend one finger at a time, thumb first, pinky last. As you do, give each finger a little bend. Notice how the joints work. It's easier to bend your fingers at the joints than it is to move them side to side.

- Now move up your entire arm and notice the difference between the movement of your elbow (bends in one direction, like the fingers) and the movement of your shoulder (a circular range of movement, like the wrist).

Biomechanical explorations like these help us begin to understand our movements at a basic level. Imagine, everything within the range of biomechanics comes down to simple movements and gestures with beginnings, middles, and ends - similar to the three-phase structure (preparation, stroke, and retraction) I mentioned at the end of Chapter 1.

There's something else at play as well, and that brings us back to deictic gestures. Earlier I asked you to imagine using a hand puppet; now, imagine that you're a marionette with strings. As a marionette, your body discovers how various joints work: how its elbows bend, how its feet flex back and forth, and so on. Staying with this idea:

- Turn your head and look off slowly to the left, then to the right.
- Pick your arm up and point to something at your right. As you do, flex your finger with the biomechanics in mind, letting each knuckle do its work.
- As you hold the gesture, turn your head back to the left. Now, adjust your gaze and let the room expand.

When you use deictic gestures onstage, or at the front of a room, your audience watches your eyes, and tracks where you look and point. Recognizing and experiencing the way that various gestures come from the body, starting with the deictics, begins to strengthen the connections between your conscious and subconscious actions. As you practice, you'll continue to gain more control over the space around you and gain new ways to convey physical messages.

We also have to include our spines as part of the biomechanical conversation. Our spines play major roles in communicating moral and emotional feelings. Interestingly, we tend to think of the spine as a whole unit. However, biomechanically, the spine is a collection of vertebrae. When we think of them as parts, we discover an entirely new range of movement and motion that most of us ignore. This biomechanical range of motion also comes into play when we consider the deictic gestures. Here are a few simple movements to demonstrate this point:

- From a seated position, rise to standing as you normally would. Repeat this movement a few times slowly, noticing the movement of your spine between your neck and pelvis. Where do you look while performing this action? How does the movement begin? How does it end?

- From a standing position, sit back down slowly. Notice how and when you shift the weight from your feet to your seat. What do you do with your eyes?

- From a seated position, look down at your toes, first just with your eyes, then allow the head and neck to follow; continue this rolling down until you can fold forward onto your legs, always looking at your toes (a succession of movement starting with the eyes).

- From there, with your eyes focused on your belly button, roll up from the base of the spine, allowing the neck and head to arrive last (the eyes still gazing at your belly). Release the eyes. Where do you settle your eyes now?

From a biomechanical perspective, we can all benefit from thinking of our bodies as marionettes, composed of parts that connect at joints. Many parts work together to create dynamic movements and poses. For instance, think of the joints in the arm from earlier: shoulder, elbow, wrist, fingers. Each individual joint must cooperate with the other joints just to make a hand gesture (a thumbs-up, for instance). Now consider the fact that we have two arms which extend from a bendable torso. All these parts add up to give you more chances to move in specific ways than most people take advantage of.

The main idea of these types of exercise is to help you start to see the relationship between posture and gestures. We'll explore this idea in Chapter 4, when we discuss how Delsarte broke down the body into a series of regions and subregions.

Chapter 3 Reflections

I wanted to start our larger conversation on the six gesture types with puppetry and biomechanics since the movement of our joints and eyes brings to life what the body does—and demonstrates what the body can do. Puppetry and biomechanics provide windows into how even very small gestures and movements resonate, and how the gestures in this book work in our corporeal instrument—the body itself.

THE BODY AS AN INSTRUMENT

Deictic gestures align with biomechanics, and refer to the way in which we see, extend, and experience the world with our eyes and pointing gestures.

- Deictics are always pointing gestures, whether we're pointing with our eyes, hands, feet, or whole body.

- Deictics help to establish the spaces we're trying to set. As performers and presenters, we're constantly setting space. In fact, wherever we look, we either set the space or open the world of our performance to a new space.

- The deictics also help us set new characters in specific spaces—whether or not the audience ever sees or hears them.

Now, think of people being people in the world. Actually, let's think of a baby again, which is where we started this chapter. Before this tiny master of deictic gestures develops muscle control to lift her arms and point, she relates to the world via her eyes and glances. And, just like our puppets, the baby doesn't know or understand social constructs or have a clue about expectations or norms. She's just there, taking it all in.

Day after day, as the baby's eyes move around, the world comes into brighter and bigger focus. Soon, she can see the mobile above her crib, then the world above the mobile. One day, her mother's smiling face lowers toward her nose. Later, the baby notices the family dog coming to lick her hand, and her eyes grow wide with a mix of excitement and uncertainty.

Her eyes stay active, and her parents track them as they go. She stares at something behind her mother's shoulder, and her mother turns around and looks. The baby's eyes have extended the world.

Soon, the baby will begin developing muscle control. First, she'll point to the thing she wants, or in the direction she wants you to take her when you're holding her. Then, she'll crawl toward it, then surf the furniture as she learns to walk. All along, her early movements will be exercises in biomechanics: she doesn't yet possess the fluidity that we eventually come to possess and use as we grow up.

Just like our puppets coming to life, the baby is simply there in the beginning. She's looking around, watching, and learning. Soon, though, what she sees will begin to appear in her body: she'll go from standing, to walking, to manipulating the objects of the world around her, often mimicking her caretakers as she steps into her life. Mimicry is where we'll go next, as we move to Chapter 4.

CHAPTER 4

What the Body Says

Chapter 3 started our conversation on the biomechanics of gestures—the micro movements that exist within movements. Now, we'll shift our exploration and look at how we mimic the physical world (iconic gesture types) and how we express the invisible world (metaphoric gesture types). To do so, we'll lean into some old theatrical forms, and explore iconic and metaphoric gestures in the process. Throughout this chapter, I'll reference the work of François Delsarte, the nineteenth-century French performer and teacher known for having developed the Delsarte method. Finally, in the reflection section I'll briefly discuss emblematic gestures, which point the way to our conversation about realism.

Showing What We Mean

Every gesture is a tool to help support our communication process, whether we are telling a story, explaining a situation, asking for help, or entertaining another person with anecdotes or funny tales. Roughly 90 percent of all gestures we use happen when we're talking, meaning that the vast majority of our gestures tend to be co-speech gestures. Certain gestures help us key in on visual elements in our words, such as size, shape, or how something is used. Often, iconic gestures help us illustrate parts of a story we're telling:

- "That dog's paws were this big." (I stretch my fingers out and hold my hand menacingly in the air.)
- "Its ears were pulled all the way back on its head." (I put my hands on either side of my head and hold them straight up like ears.)
- "It stared at me for a second, like it wanted to eat me for lunch." (I squint and hold a mean gaze for a few seconds as I talk.)

Then, as we're telling our story, it's natural for iconic gestures to give way to hyperbole, or downright comedy:

- "I mean, that Corgi was huge!" (I spread my arms wide at the word "huge.")
- "She ran so hard to get that bouquet." (I pump my arms as though I'm running, even though I'm sitting in a chair as I retell the story.)
- "And I mean she was *really* running." (I make a finger-person who runs along my arm.)
- "But then she jumped (Gesture: the finger-person jumps) and landed next to a big pile of snakes." (Gesture: finger-person lands on table, my fingers are now wiggling.)

These gestures aren't just random gesticulations. They are specific physical parts of communicating the story—any story—we're telling. As a speaker, they help to embellish or clarify the story for your audience. At the same time, their presence in the telling may have more to do with physically processing the images that our brains produce. They extend the visual imagery without slowing down the narrative. Whatever the case may be, the way we enact them has a distinct relationship with mime and pantomime.

Mimicry and Mime

Mime is all about mimicry and imitation. When Livius Andronicus lost his voice, his gestures took over in a direct and intentional way. No longer possessing the ability to speak, he used his body to mimic and replicate what he and his audience knew from the world around them.

Recall that our baby from Chapter 3 began to discover the world through her eyes. Over time, as she made sense of what she saw, she shaped and extended the world through various deictic gestures—glances, points, nods, etc. Now, through mimicry, she will begin to recreate things within her world and discover the meanings of things by imitating what she sees, hears, and internalizes.

As the child develops, she starts to imitate other people and things she sees in her environment. One day, she watches her mother have a tense phone call with a friend. Later, the child puts a banana to one of her ears, and, while toddling around a bit, mimics her mother's posture, and even flaps her hands and mutters to an imaginary friend on the other end.

Modern mime and pantomime present moments when we reach beyond ourselves to grab, shape, and create objects, animals, or people that exist strictly in the gestures of our bodies. However, when we reach beyond ourselves and imitate those things, our audience understands what noun we are attempting to communicate since we show how it exists (as a verb) in the world. Like that young child, we choose a body position that we intend to physically represent the person or thing. Then, the gestures emanate from that posture, which adds details to the imitation.

To give an example of this, we turn to Charles Aubert, a French pantomimist from the nineteenth century. In order to mimic people and animals, our body naturally adds itself to the gesture image, such as a king or a snake. If you mimic your teacher, you may lift your shoulders with a slight shake, while extending a wagging finger and asking, "Are you paying attention?" How would you mimic an object? We usually do so with our hands. For instance, if you mime a pen, you most likely mimic the act of writing, using just your hand to enact the verb. What is your body doing? What if you add more of your body to the gesture? First, set your posture to imitate the pen, then gesture a pen with your hand, to write. It should bring more embodiment (and size) to your iconic gestures. Try it with "piano" (to play), or "coffee cup" (to drink).

Granted, not everyone is a mime—actually, very few of us are. Still, seeing how gestures create verbs and show action can help us animate our stories in a new style the next time we share them. Now, I'd like to illustrate a few ways that iconic and metaphoric gestures show up in our daily conversations.

Using Iconic and Metaphoric Gestures

When you're using an iconic gesture, you're essentially trying to replicate or copy from the known world. Elsewhere in this book, I've referenced things like:

- Trying to open a stuck jar.
- Looking for scissors.
- A dog's physical features.

I've also mentioned a young child imitating her mother's conversation by turning a banana into a telephone. This is how we know the world: through our bodies, via our physical and empirical senses. When we lean into iconic gestures, we naturally mimic the concepts we need to include in a story, anecdote, or scenario at play. It's really the only way we can.

On the other side of this equation, we find our metaphoric gestures, which arrive just in time to help us show an abstract concept, thought, or emotion. We touch our heart (emotion), pat down the air (minimize, decrease, lessen), or present two imagined entities in the space that hold opposing concepts (this and that). Whether in an iconic or a metaphoric context, we're often in the midst of explaining an idea or a subset of content that's attached to the idea.

If you and I were to meet in a café, our conversation might be fifteen, twenty, perhaps forty-five minutes long, complete with pauses, starts, stops, restarts…the entire gamut of person-to-person communication. I'll talk, you'll talk, we'll talk over each other by accident, and the whole time we'll be making gestures toward and away from each other over the table. Our words won't move inside of the space—words never move in a space, since they have no mass. But our bodies will occupy that dimension and fill the spatial element with the mass and gravity our words lack.

To a large degree, this is what iconic and metaphoric gestures are doing: responding to various items or content while we're speaking, nearly becoming entities of the ideas themselves. Here's an example of how we think our ideas out physically and how we use metaphoric gestures in our everyday lives: Even when the people we're talking with can't see our gestures, we're still gesturing in space for ourselves. Don't believe it? Try it for yourself. The next time you have a hands-free phone call with someone, describe your favorite odor and keep track of what your hands are doing when you're talking. Unless you glue your hands to your legs, they will most likely be moving. Now, some people may consider this to be evidence that you're just someone who "talks with their hands." Maybe that's right, but neurologically speaking, your hands, as an extension of thought, are creating a spatial representation of the objects you're talking about (iconic) or occupying a space for an emotion or abstract idea (metaphoric).

At the end of the day, iconic and metaphoric gestures synchronize with the idea you're trying to convey. Whether they present an image of something we know of in the world (iconic), or an abstraction (metaphoric), they typically operate in direct relation to our thought, memory, or idea.

Where These Gestures Live Spatially

When considering the iconic gestures we use, whether in performance or everyday conversation, they tend to emanate from what McNeill calls the "center-center space."

In conversation, there's often an intimacy or closeness in relation to how we discuss nouns, and these movements tend to live and move forward from between our shoulders, as if we are extending something. Consider the following conversational sentences and the gestures that might accompany them:

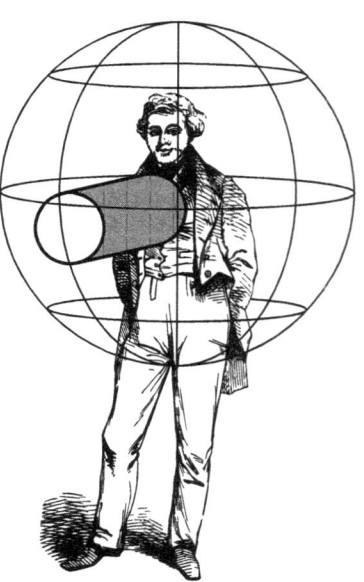

- "And then she just handed me the keys." (I hand over an imaginary set of keys to the person with whom I'm speaking; or I dangle an imaginary set of keys.)

- "I really need a spoon to eat this pie." (I stare at the pie in front of me and eat with an imaginary spoon close to the plate.)

Metaphors, on the other hand, tend to come from what he calls the "lower-center" space. Typically, when we're speaking in metaphor, and using metaphorical gestures, we have the tendency to be a little more dramatic than when we're discussing real things (as with iconic gestures). In the process, there might be more of a sweep of our gestures, and we extend our movements up beyond the center-center space to form something of a container (like a bowl) underneath and around the iconic space.

For example:

- "Thinking about those keys was so stressful." [The focus is no longer on the keys (iconic), but on the burden (abstract) that happens when you think of the keys, which the body imitates in gesture (arms drop and hands open out at the sides, to demonstrate the metaphorical weight they carry)].

- "My goodness, this pie tastes like heaven." (My arm pumps its palm up, next to my head, trying my best to physically showcase the sublime. Meanwhile, my neck even dances a little for joy.)

These Gestures Can Help Us Organize Our Thinking

One of the ways we use iconic and metaphoric gestures in everyday conversation is to help organize our thinking or set anchor points in a conversation (different from the anchors we set with deictics, which are about creating anchors in space via distance). With iconic and metaphoric gestures, the anchors we create are more about thoughts, topics, plot points, and various aspects related to a conversation or story we're telling in the space surrounding us. We can think of this as creating something of a synchronicity between what we're saying and what we're showing: the gestures provide additional information that goes beyond what our words convey.

- You and your friend are trying to decide whether to drive to the beach or go to the mountains for a hike. As you do your best to weigh the pros and cons, you get your hands involved in the conversation. "We can either have a day of sand and sunshine," (undulating motions in your arms, you extend your left hand, your palm and fingers imitating waves, to represent the beach idea) "or green trees and shade." (You extend your right hand in a chopping motion extending your neck to represent the forest idea.)

- Holding the end of the gesture, you continue: "They're both good options on this summer day." (With open palms, you tip your hands like scales.)

- As you sit there with both hands out and open, your friend stares back at your hands. Your gesture has brought her into the physical representation of both places. As she stares, you continue your part of the conversation: "I'm really leaning toward the beach." (You undulate your hand and imitate the motion in your neck.)

- Your friend looks a little more intently at your right hand now. "Yeah, but I could really use a trip to the mountains. Let's do that!" (She points to your right hand, straightens her neck, and makes a quick little chopping motion with her hand.) Still holding the end of the gesture, she adds, "I need some quiet serenity today."

The interesting thing about this example is that if we take the words away, we still see a choice being offered. With the help of the nouns (beach and mountains), the gestures enhance the words with feelings/ideas of those destinations. At the same time, without the gestures, perhaps it would take longer to clarify the idea. "Hmmm, why should we go to the beach? The mountains? Wait, why do you want to go again? I'm confused."

In addition, if you and your friend come back to this conversation later in the day, the reference points or orientational metaphors still hold. So, if you notice your friend packing a bag and she grabs her towel and sunscreen, instead of her walking sticks and bug spray, you might hold out your left hand and say, "Wait, so it's beach now?"

These Gestures Can Also Help Us Communicate Where

Iconic and metaphoric gestures also help us demonstrate where things exist in time and space. Lakoff and Johnson cover a lot of ground related to spatial orientation throughout the book *Metaphors We Live By*. Often, spatial orientations dovetail with words we're speaking:

- "We need to be more proud." (Here a metaphoric expression mixes with a corresponding gesture, such as lifting your hands, palms up, from stomach to chest.)
- "We'll worry about that later." (Here the gesture moves forward from the body into the space before us that occupies our idea of future/forward.)

- Often gestures for the past will pass toward or behind us: "We did that yesterday." (The hand passes over the shoulder.)
- We may gesture outside/in when talking about receiving, witnessing, or having an experience, and reverse the direction when discussing ideas of rejection, stopping, or negating something.
- If we enjoy something or have elation, the gesture often moves up, and the opposite for sadness or rejection.
- Groups/family/community ideas can often be seen in circles or arcs, and a breaking apart gesture when discussing betrayal, or infidelity.
- "He was lost, but now he's found." As a way to show progression, transformation, etc., we may present these ideas in the same direction in which we read: left to right. And vice versa if someone returns, goes back, undoes, or reverses something.

When in conversation, these gestures help communicate abstract thoughts and structure the way we share complex ideas. In addition to the cardinal directions above, here is a short list of primary images that we often see in our gestures, especially when discussing philosophy or religion or politics or math.[8]

---

8 Mark Johnson, *The Body in the Mind*, (Chicago, University of Chicago Press, 1987), 125, Kindle.

Container	Path	Scale
Balance	Link	Merging
Blockage	Center-Periphery	Splitting
Counterforce	Cycle	Contact
Restraint Removal	Near-Far	Surface Collection

We're constantly delivering gestures through a variety of these structure types. Sometimes these structures present the idea or argument. For instance, after we leave the doctor's office, you and I are arguing about the doctor's advice:

- Gesture: a hand makes a forward circle: "No! He said you have to start with the diet and exercise first! Then you return to see the doctor." (Gesture: flitting downward) "And if the doctor says it's okay, then you can enter the pie-eating contest!"

- Gesture: the hands in parallel, move right-left in front of the body, as if to remove an entity or fog: "You can't think like that anymore; we're going to prove him wrong. Just watch."

- Gesture: the hand moves in stages from the center to the periphery: "You start off taking a small dose, and then she'll adjust your medication, and then we go to the surgeon, before we go to Costa Rica."

Even as we're talking, we're illustrating the shape of our narrative, thought, or idea through the visual of our gestures. Now, as it relates to the energy, size, speed, and frequency of the gestures we use, the conversation shifts over to François Delsarte.

Delsarte's Influence on Gestures

Delsarte was a leading name in the world of gestures and performance in the middle of the nineteenth century. For him, the gestures, especially metaphoric ones, were instrumental in delivering meaning. As he saw things, there were certain laws that governed the aesthetics of human movement and communication. If you were a student of Delsarte who'd been chased by a dog, you might do the following:

- Place both hands on a table to start...
- Speak over your shoulder...
- Deliver short, quick gestures from the chest, while talking about having been chased by the dog.
- Then, turning your body (nearly 180 degrees), keep your hands on the table, but with the angle inverted, arch your back and then...

- Making a slow gesture to the head, explain how you triumphantly arrived at the house before the dog bit you.

To work from Delsarte's perspective for a moment:

- The whole body combines to create an expression and show changes in emotion.
- The bend in the torso corresponds with a change in the attitude of the character, something like exhaustion or fear (a person bends over the table) or the body changes to show triumph or pride (an arching of the spine).
- Meanwhile, the gestures extend from those spinal positions.
- In this example, the frequency of the gesture can communicate the energy of the emotion.

The speed and shape of these gestures, accompanied by spoken language, manifest Delsarte's aesthetic:

- You and your friend are talking, and there's a word that's escaping her. If it's a big deal, she might show anger at herself (the speed of the gesture may be slow and deliberate); if it's not a big deal, she might be relaxed about it (the speed of the gesture may be fluid and quick).

WHAT THE BODY SAYS

- The two of you are sitting at a table. You lean forward, anticipating what she's about to say. Your friend looks down at the table, then into space, then up at the ceiling. "It was…uh…it was right here in my head!" If she's angry at herself, she might press or even softly slap the side of her temple to dislodge or jostle the memory. Or if she's relaxed about it, she might just snap her fingers and brush her hand in the air to suggest coaxing the memory back into her head.

Delsarte's method was a way for students to improve their expression through their use of gestures, using a type of biomechanics. In his own career as a performer, Delsarte was a singer who lost his voice from bad training at the conservatory. Similar to Livius Andronicus, Delsarte turned to expression in the body, since the voice could no longer express it in song.

Students of Delsarte's method came to understand various scientific and biomechanical aspects of the body: how parts of the body broke down into smaller parts; how gestures could help exaggerate various emotions. From this foundation, they developed and delivered a range of movements that often equated to high emotional stakes: big movements meant really big emotions or were necessary to truly deliver meaning to audiences over low-lit, long distance. Today, of course, we might consider such movements to be overly exaggerated, or purposely, even ironically melodramatic. For example, the exaggerated faint places the back of the hand on the forehead, before the body falls sideways.

Delsarte had a number of famous students during his time, but you may recognize Delsarte's technique through the work of Sarah Bernhardt, the most iconic and recognizable actress of her day. Known as the literal "queen of the pose" and "the princess of the gesture," Bernhardt even played male characters, including Hamlet. When we study images of Bernhardt today, it's easy to see Delsarte's influence, from the way she affected whole-body poses to the largesse and emotional displays present in her work as she externally expressed a full spectrum of internalized feelings.

Discussing Delsarte today presents some interesting challenges. For one, he never wrote a book, which leaves no primary text to explore. At the same time, having applied meaning to various gestures, Delsarte had a direct hand in creating a system of codification related to the gestures. For instance, he instructed his students to position their feet this way, and the spine that way, and to deliver various gestures in a spiral in order to create specific expressions. On an even more granular level, he charted various positions for the eyebrows, eyes, and fingers in order to show a range of emotions, even codifying combinations for specific expressions. It wasn't much different from what Cicero and Quintilian had done in their time for public speaking and oration. Focused on public performance, Delsarte was looking to define expressive language through physical movement. Even though there was no primary text to refer to, many of his students continued to reinterpret his codification for years after his death.

At the core of Delsarte's focus was muscular tension, triggering emotions by flexing certain physical states that would connect the actor to the emotion. In his view, putting the body into various physical forms could do a lot of the emotional work for the actor. Teachers and performers were still using variations of the Delsarte method until Russian realism found its way to America in the early 1920s.

Zones of the Body

For Delsarte, the body was a triad (divided into thirds) with a head, an upper body, and a lower body. He noticed relationships existed within these zones and built a system codifying different combinations that he found to influence expressions and attitudes. He also noticed how the zones, as a whole, created something of a harmonic balance, and to apply an understanding of them could improve the quality of postures.

Organizing the body into thirds was just the beginning of Delsarte's training. His system further divided each zone into triads, allowing movement variations to be codified down to extreme details related to various combinations that involved the head, neck, torso, arms, hands and fingers, legs, and feet. Here's an image to help you get a better sense of Delsarte's zones of the body, and how he broke various zones into triads as well:[9]

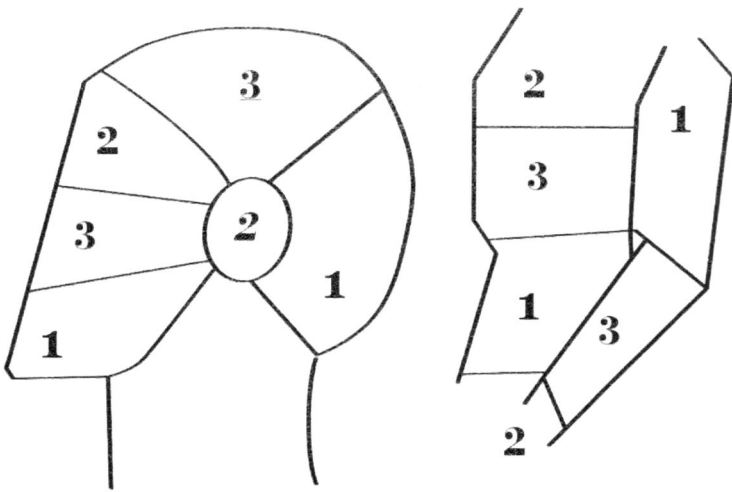

L'Abbe Delaumosne, *Zones of the Head, Face and Arm*, 1882, illustration, *The Art of Oratory: System of Delsarte*.

The following pages show some additional examples of Delsarte's codification of the eyes and hands for reference.[10]

---

9 L'Abbe Delaumosne, *The Art of Oratory: System of Delsarte*, trans. Frances A. Shaw (Albany: Edgar S. Werner, 1882), 109.
10 Delaumosne, *Art of Oratory*, 74; Delaumosne, *Art of Oratory*, 94.

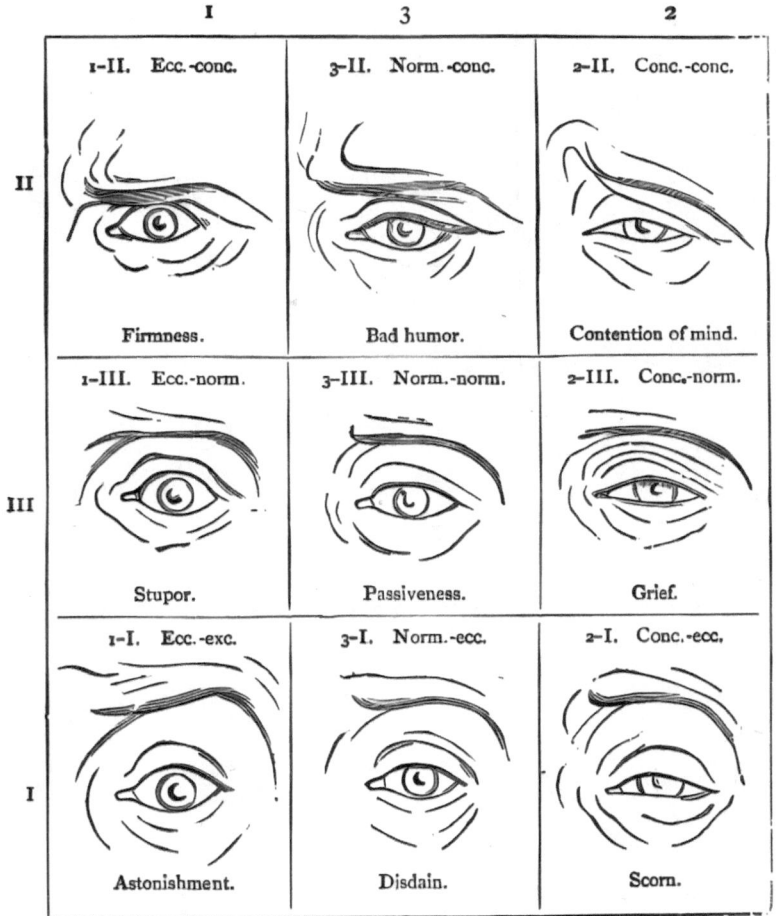

L'Abbe Delaumosne, *Criterion of the Eyes*, 1882, illustration, *The Art of Oratory: System of Delsarte*.

YOUR VISUAL CONNECTION

CRITERION OF THE HAND.

	1	3	2
I	1-II. Ecc.-conc. — Convulsive.	3-II. Norm.-conc. — Tonic or power.	2-II. Conc.-conc. — Conflict.
III	1-III. Ecc.-norm. — Expansive.	3-III. Norm.-norm. — Abandon.	2-III. Conc.-norm. — Prostration.
II	1-I. Ecc.-ecc. — Exasperation.	3-I. Norm.-ecc. — Exaltation.	2-I. Conc.-ecc. — Retraction.

L'Abbe Delaumosne, *Criterion of the Hand*, 1882, illustration, *The Art of Oratory: System of Delsarte*.

I'd also like to share some examples of how Delsarte's system of codification related to various zones, as well as the zones within zones:

- Movements associated with the head (brain) connected with thought, or mental and intellectual acumen.
- Movements from the upper torso (heart) related to emotions, morality, or spiritual yearning. They could suggest a wide range of emotions, including courage, love, hunger, passion, and other feelings.
- Meanwhile, movements in the lower torso are related to vitality or the energy of being alive and present, as well as carnal appetites and desires.

Going deeper into the study and understanding of various zones of the body, we also can see how they support three orders of movement: opposition, parallelism, and succession.

- Opposition: any two parts of the body moving in opposite directions simultaneously.
- Parallelism: two parts of the body moving simultaneously in the same direction.
- Succession: movements that receive and pass their origin through the body (as a wave moves).

Here are a few visual references to help illustrate the orders of movement. You'll also find some exercises in Chapter 8 that refer back to Delsarte and the zonal study of the body.

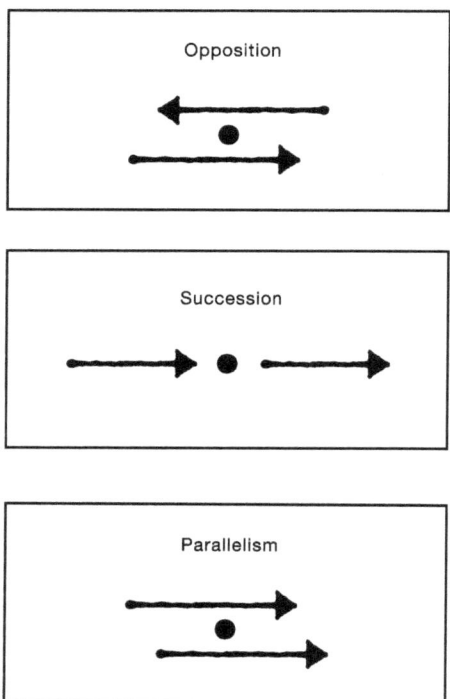

Today, I believe there's value in keeping Delsarte in the conversation of gestures and performance. Staying with his triad concept, the legs and feet make interesting areas to explore in the present day. Very few acting coaches will talk about your feet. In fact, when we're in front of a group of people, we rarely think about our feet at all. When I'm in an audience, I try to look at an actor's legs and feet as a way to gauge how present they are in the performance—and in their own bodies for that matter. Are they actually performing or presenting with their whole body, or just from the neck up?[11]

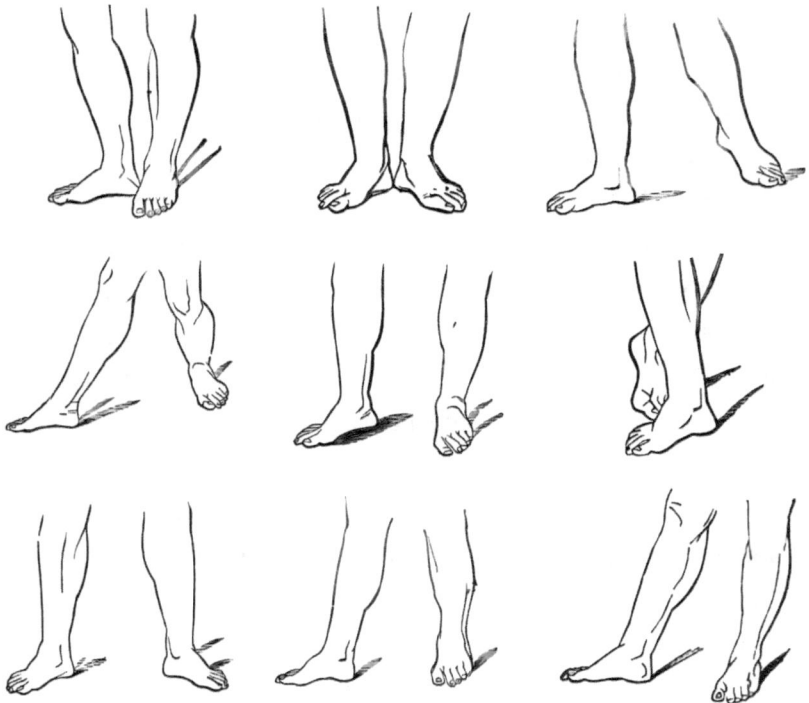

L'Abbe Delaumosne, *Attitudes of the Legs*, 1882, illustration, *The Art of Oratory: System of Delsarte*.

---

11   Delaumosne, *Art of Oratory*, 101–106.

This brings to mind podiums again, those power blockers that seem right at home during just about any political speech or debate we watch, except for sit-down, town hall conversations. Standing behind a podium makes it easier for us to control our behavior and keeps an audience from seeing what our feet and legs are doing. We don't have to worry about that half of our body at all, or about our legs and feet distracting anyone. That way, the audience can focus on our words, along with our facial and hand gestures.

Let's go back to the three orders of movement (opposition, parallelism, and succession). Together, they represent another aspect of Delsarte's teaching that remains prevalent today. Through opposition, parallelism, and succession, a performer can intentionally set the body and gestures in ways that suggest balance, tension, progression, and retraction—even oscillating between tensions at different times. Opposition especially shows up in a great deal of Bernhardt's work and relates to ways and times in which we can take greater advantage of the body's biomechanical range in order to extend the nature of the physical narratives we seek to tell.

An Exercise for Metaphoric Gestures

For a presenter, politician, or anyone who needs to briefly take the stage or stand in the spotlight, it's worth spending some time thinking about the form that your body takes at different times. Consider:

- Confidence: your chest lifts, shoulders drop.
- Power: your chest lifts, shoulders tense.
- Surprised: your chest leans back, hands open at your side.
- Fear: your chest leans back, hands out in front.
- Sadness: your chest down, shoulders drop.

Throughout this chapter, as we discussed metaphoric gestures, the gestures tended to emanate from specific zones of the body:

- Upper: gestures about confusion, vision, thinking, etc.
- Middle: gestures about passion, feeling, love, etc.
- Lower: gestures about secrecy, appetites, sex, etc.

The exercise I've chosen to share focuses on body posture, and works through a series of stances and ranges before adding gestures:

- First, find a reflective service (a mirror, window, etc.) where you can see your torso, but not your head. If you have a full-length mirror, you can tape paper or cardboard to the top portion, so you only see your torso, but not your head.

- Standing in front of your mirror or other reflective surface, let your arms go limp, so they're just dangling at the sides of your body, relax and "be yourself." This is your "authentic" self (the version of yourself you believe you physically carry around and present to the world every day).

- Now, using only your legs, torso and spine, begin to mimic or imitate the following persona types:
    - Someone showing courage
    - Someone showing self-doubt

- Next, let's do some oscillation:
    - Oscillate from courage to self-doubt, then back to courage
    - From courage, move to someone showing passion; then to indifference
    - From indifference, move to beauty; then to ugliness
    - Come back to courage, then to your authentic self

Notice the turns and bends your spine goes through as you posture each expression. This exercise can also be something you return to again and again as a way to recalibrate your "authentic" posture. Now to add the arms and hands. Incorporating gestures can enhance the outward expression of these postures. Remember to set the body first, before you supply the gestures. Try it first just with the ones I've listed above, before moving onto these:

- Wisdom
- Boredom
- Wonder
- Creativity
- Ordinariness

As you move through this exercise, track the changes your body goes through. What happens with your legs? Where is there opposition, parallelism, and/or succession in your body? Also, what's happening with your face? Even though you can't see your face in this exercise, does it help if you make your facial expression really big? Can you feel that change in your legs?

One way to take this exercise to a new level is to record yourself while you're doing it, and then watch the recording later so as to study and build upon your movements. Many of my theatre students add the recording element, especially when they're considering ways to enhance their physical performance style.

Chapter 4 Reflections

We already possess all the gestures we need to carry on a conversation. We've been picking up these gestures since our earliest memories and have been building a library with the help of the connection that exists between our brains and bodies.

As children, we learn through mimicking the people and objects around us. Walking is one of the first places where mimicry shows up, as some children will even adopt the gait of their primary caretaker. As adults, when we mimic someone, we mimic their dynamics, rhythms, velocity, speed… everything. It could be their posture, facial expressions, or even the intonation of their voice.

In the process of mimicking, we explore various iconic gestures, building our way into a new physical vocabulary. These gestures present visual interpretations of things that exist in the world. Meanwhile, various metaphorical gestures reside close to the surface as we tell stories, illustrate abstract thoughts, or try to convey a universal idea. Quite often, we'll lean into iconic and metaphoric gestures in an almost point-by-point manner as we're retelling a funny story to a friend or engaging with just about any audience.

Here are a few key points to help iron out the finer details of iconic and metaphoric gesture types:

- An iconic gesture relates to our physical world (person, thing, or action).
- However, through mime, we learn that nouns are demonstrated using verbal gestures: "a pen," which equals the verb "to write"; "a friend," which equals

"to be friendly, kind and inviting"; "a painter," which equals "to paint"; etc.
- Meanwhile, metaphoric gestures help express feelings, attitudes, thoughts, and ideas ("He played the piano too loudly, he was so angry while he played."

With the help of biomechanics, which we first discussed in Chapter 3, we continue to expand the way we communicate via the gestures we use. Recognizing biomechanics quantifies the speed and posture of our body and impacts how much energy we bring to our gestures.

There's one more gesture type to bring up here as we reflect on Chapter 4: emblematic. These are the gestures that we carry around and use fairly casually. They often fill in for natural speech in our everyday lives: the way we wave as we walk toward the dais at the front of the room; flashing a peace sign to a friend; a thumbs-up sign to let someone know we're doing alright. Since they're linked to words, we even find emblems in hand emojis these days: sending a "prayer hands" or "thumbs-down" gesture to someone from smartphone to smartphone, for example.

Within a culture, no one misunderstands the meaning of an emblematic gesture. They possess and communicate language. Emblematic gestures have a connection to the notion of codification I've been mentioning since Cicero and Quintilian and must be performed in a specific way. For the most part, these gesture types say "exactly X" when I do "exactly Y." In fact, emblematic gestures are the most codified of all these gesture types, in that their meaning is specific to cultural use.

Many emblematic gestures start off as either iconic or metaphoric gestures, for example, the classic knuckle tapping several times on a wooden surface. Here's a brief track of its evolution:

- It was thought that jealous tree spirits would try to destroy good luck if they heard one talk of happiness. Touching an oak tree would placate those spirits (action), as their roots were thought to descend into the underworld.

- Soon, however, "knocking on wood" came to mean "protection" (metaphoric) accompanied with an actual knock on the wood (iconic interpretation of action).

- Over time, the metaphorical meaning became known as a "good luck" gesture. Today, people readily use it in public, rather than privately. Quite often, people don't even bother saying "knock on wood," but instead just make the gesture: "He's feeling much better now (gesture: knock on wood)."

With emblematic gestures, the emotion and meaning come through in a culturally consistent way. It's important to note here, as we begin to wrap up Chapter 4, that emblematic gestures actually point the way forward to realism.

Realism isn't concerned with biomechanics and does not leave much room for gestures. In fact, realism asks you to do away with gestures in favor of actions. That's why if we saw Sarah Bernhardt today, we might think she was overacting—it's a fact of our modern conditioning where gestures are concerned. We might enjoy what she does, but we'd find everything she did unrealistic: too heavy, over-stylized, and completely overly dramatic.

But perhaps the gestural tide is shifting some, especially as we look for ways to adapt our techniques and create stronger connections. That's my hope, and that's where I'd like to take the conversation as we move to Chapter 5.

CHAPTER 5

Gestures and Reality

Within the context of realism, rehearsed or forced gestures can destroy the image of naturalism. Gestures in performance are urged to be natural and spontaneous, arriving out of the emotion in that moment. But what does this mean? In spontaneous conversations, we often use one gesture per clause, but when does it naturally occur?

Try this as a little experiment using some text: "His stare… it makes me nervous" (The gesture: both hands, fingers splayed, fanning the neck):

- sync the gesture (stroke) on the word "nervous"

- now, slightly un-sync the gesture (stroke) with the same word
- finally, perform the whole gesture and hold it as you say the line

Which is more "real" or spontaneous? Does one feel more deliberate or performative? Adam Kendon noticed in casual conversations that the stroke of a gesture was often completed either before or on, but not after, the peak syllable of the "utterance."[12] This is good to know if you prefer to rehearse your gestures, because this one small adjustment can bring them back into any natural performance genre: boardroom, stage play, or Zoom call.

But what makes realism unique in performance is the affect gesture type. Emblematic and affect gesture types exist on opposite ends of the performance gesture scale. Where emblems are concerned, these gestures literally stand in for words. On the other end, affect gestures fill in the space between spontaneous gestures to create realism, and disappear in pantomime in order to obey form and style.

The notion is that as your physical gestures become more precise, the more meaningful your communication. Obviously, that depends on the person more than anything, and it's far from being an absolute in the world

---

12 Kendon, Gesture: Visible Action as Utterance.

of performance. Specific to this chapter, we'll look at what realism means during presentations and performances and discuss ways in which characterizations become real as you work to embody and own the space around you.

We'll start our conversation where we left off in Chapter 4, with emblematic gestures, then make our way to affect gestures, and the roles they play when we're performing.

Emblematic Gestures

Emblematic gestures carry more cultural history than other gestures do. In fact, the most well-known gestures tend to be emblematic—the ones we see most often, and the easiest to recognize. We've all seen and used emblematic gestures: the thumb to the nose; the middle finger; the peace sign; the hook 'em horns. But have we explored how the meaning of gestures changes across cultures? Did you know, for instance, that the casual peace sign many of us throw around in the U.S. actually means something quite vulgar in the U.K. if you flip it around? Or that the hook 'em horns might mean one thing if you're a fan of University of Texas football, but in Europe it means something dramatically different within the context of relationships and infidelity?

In certain ways, emblematic gestures are closer to sign language than are the other five gesture types, as they literally stand in for words or phrases.

- People often make emblematic gestures with their hands or arms. It doesn't require much action for an emblematic gesture to get its point across.

- Emblems don't accompany speech, since they are a physical manifestation of a word, phrase, or idea. Many emblems are easy to understand from a distance: you don't need to be too close to convey your message, which is a good thing, since many emblems are offensive in nature.

- Emblematic gestures are rooted in their origins, and some are the remains of old iconic gestures or actions. All emblems are culturally specific (possessing an indigenous meaning). As Desmond Morris writes, "What is polite in one region is obscene in another. What is friendly here, is hostile there. That is why a guide is needed."[13]

- Emblematic gestures always follow the three-phase structure I mentioned earlier in the book. With emblematics, however, the preparation happens a little quicker, and most of the gesture's attention falls

---

13 Desmond Morris, *Bodytalk. A World Guide to Gestures*, (London, Jonathan Cape, 1994), Introduction.

on the stroke. Quickly flipping the middle finger or a thumbs-up are two classic examples.

In Chapter 4, I shared that emblematic gestures often begin as iconic or metaphorical gestures, or a series of gestures that truncate over time, finally becoming one distinct motion:

- For instance, I can screw my forefinger against my temple to suggest that someone "has a screw loose." A more involved version of this same gesture might include tapping my temple several times and making a puzzled face. Here, the first example is emblematic (stands for phrase), and the second is metaphoric (impersonation of internal state).

- Using another example from Chapter 4, a child turned a banana into a telephone. When she's a little older (middle school), she turns her hand into a phone as she passes her friend in the hallway, and without even mouthing "call me," the friend understands. In this case, the iconic has become emblematic.

Using Emblematic Gestures in Performance

For actors, emblematic gestures take on different meanings in a performance, based on a few things: how often we repeat them; the speed and force with which we use them; and whether or not we use them in a way that's culturally correct and understood. For instance:

- A shy character flips off the bully, while smiling a "see you tomorrow" look. We can consider this an "emblematic slip," where the verbal message contradicts the gesture.
- Shaking your head no while saying "absolutely not." We'd consider this to be a "pure emblematic," as the gesture aligns with the meaning behind it.

Here are a few other examples of emblematic gestures where a performer can incorporate an emblematic slip, or create a level of friction or cognitive dissonance between the gestures and the words:

- Shaking your head "no" while saying "yes." (Or the opposite: nodding "yes" while saying "no.")
- The raised "yes" eyebrows while saying "no"; the scrunched "no" face while saying "yes."
- Shoulder shrug ("I don't know") while speaking an affirmative answer.

And here are a few extra examples of pure emblematic gestures, which you can use without words to help your character get your point across:

GESTURES AND REALITY

- Your two open palms facing up in a classic "I don't know," when you truly don't know.
- Dropping your shoulders and exhaling as a sign of relief, while rolling your eyes so as to say "whatever."
- Sticking your tongue out childishly, while humming "na-na-nuh-na-na-nuh."

As a member of the audience, if we see a character use an emblematic gesture that we do not recognize, we're left without any meaning or reference. However, when we see a different character respond to the emblem, it opens us up to new levels of understanding. We get what's going on, regardless of whether or not either character says a word. This two-way conversation takes place via the conduit of a single gesture, and replicates something familiar we recognize from real life.

The meaning of an emblematic gesture also comes across via speed, force, and size. My earlier example of making a classic "screw loose" gesture toward my temple illustrates this point. If I had quickened (and lengthened) the gesture or used an open palm (rather than a finger), then the suggestion would be different. And, since emblems rely on a mutually agreed use, you might not have understood the meaning of my gesture, unless I added words.

For a performer, emblematic gestures should only be used out of context if the audience has an advanced understanding of the reference. Otherwise, the audience needs to learn the meaning of the gesture.

- The meaning of emblematic gestures doesn't change, but the emphasis of the meaning changes depending on how a character uses them. There's a scene in an episode of the animated program, *Rick and Morty*, that helps to illustrate my point. In the scene, Rick tells Morty to flip off an alien crowd, because he told them the gesture means "peace among worlds."[14]

- Here's an example of a private emblematic gesture: when signing off at the end of each episode of her old variety show, Carol Burnett liked to send a personalized emblematic "tug on the ear" to her grandmother. This gesture sent a special message that only the family understood.

Emblematic gestures share an interesting dynamic with affect gestures. Of the six gesture types this book focuses on, emblematic and affect are the two non-verbal types, which makes them excellent for deceit. Emblems send specifically

---

14 Rick and Morty, "The Ricks Must Be Crazy," HBO Max, 4:30, August 30, 2015.

chosen signals that people within certain cultures or subcultures understand, whereas affect gestures send subconscious and unintentional signals that people tend to understand in a more general sense. Depending on how you use emblematic gestures (speed, frequency, vigor, etc.), they can become a character's identifying traits: the character who's always flipping people off, or who only makes certain gestures when she's around her family. The same possibilities exist with affect gestures. In fact, a character's identifying traits can be found in both emblematic gestures and affect gestures. Both possibilities can exist in performance, but only our affect gestures occur naturally in life.

Affect Gestures in Life and Performance

When you know and use the gestures, your moments onstage, on-screen, or during any type of performance are well within your grasp of control. It doesn't matter if you are standing behind a podium, a table at your friend's wedding with a microphone in your hand, or presenting a new business initiative via a video conference. Affect gestures are the non-verbal cues and communication tics we are constantly giving, whether we know them or not.

Our bodies are constantly giving away clues to our emotional, mental, and physiological states. Some things we simply cannot control. For instance:

- A racing pulse when we're excited or nervous.
- Dilating pupils when stressed or aroused.

Then there are the types of physical responses some of us learn to control over time. For instance:

- A voice that cracks or quivers when we're nervous.
- A nervous tic when we're stressed.
- Tightening or tensing of our mouths when we're upset.

All these bodily responses, and many more, fall into the fairly broad category of affect gestures. People who read behavior, body language, or non-verbal communication (NVC) will often key in on them at different times, and for different reasons. For instance, an investigator, detective, or an extremely involved doctor or therapist will attempt to connect dots between body movement and a person's mental state. Plenty of researchers have been in the process of studying and attempting to codify affect gestures for years. What kind of clues are people giving? What does it mean when people touch their noses when they answer a question? Are they lying, or do they just have an itch? Wait—they did it again, but this time when they said the word "blue."

As Michael Argyle writes in the book *Bodily Communication*, "Gestures, postures, and bodily movements are the second channel for emotion."[15] Meanwhile, Desmond Morris spins the thought of affect gestures back to the way we can learn to hide or conceal them when he writes that:

> ...general body posture can give some valuable clues... But the value of these body postures is greatly reduced by social rules that require certain rather stereotyped poses in specific contexts.[16]

Here are some other details about affect gestures I'd like to share, with a little help from Morris's work:

- They are more often than not connected to deceit. Knowing this, NVC experts will examine affect gestures in order to discern what's known as "non-verbal leakage."

- If you're an actor, then you're in one of the few, if not the only discipline where you'll want to study affect gestures in order to actually put them to use. Other disciplines (politicians, public speakers, doctors, etc.) will study affect gestures in order to learn how to control them.

---

15 Michael Argyle, *Bodily Communication*, (Madison CT, International Universities Press, 1988), 77.
16 Morris, *Manwatching*, 106.

- Speaking of controlling them: it's easier to control affect gestures that occur in some areas and zones of the body than in others. For instance, controlling a facial emotion is something you can learn to do over time, considering how conscious we are of our faces. However, it's harder to control what we do with our feet, mainly because our minds are rarely on our feet. (Hence the podium when speaking in public.)

- Finally, the most common self-touch occurs at the jaw or chin area of our faces. (Have you ever tried to count how often you touch your jaw or chin while talking?)

To Control or Not to Control

When you're speaking in public, running for office, giving a presentation, or otherwise trying to present thoughts or ideas, you probably want to control affect gestures as much as possible—unless a certain gesture is part of your schtick (like Steve Jobs in his black turtleneck rubbing his chin). You're most likely familiar with the term "polished," as if to say, "Politician X is extremely polished." This often refers to his or her lack of affect gestures, or a control of the gestures while talking—even while listening to an opponent talk or taking questions from a moderator.

GESTURES AND REALITY

TV personalities, especially newscasters and talk show hosts, will also present a fairly controlled physical manner. You may see them use beats as they're talking or form their hands in iconic or metaphorical gestures at different times, but you most likely won't see them scratch or touch their faces on TV.

Interpreting affect gestures, or using them for deceit, are interesting studies, but are not the focus of this book. Instead, I want to keep our focus on the fact that affect gestures present fertile ground in which you can explore, practice, and incorporate their use in character development. Meanwhile, for a polished presenter, knowing what affect gestures are can help you eliminate or at least minimize them when you're at the front of a room.

Like it or not, our affect gestures do carry emotional meaning, regardless of whether we're conscious of them. Often, affect gestures are the body's way of self-soothing, calming the nerves, or coping with stress. Rubbing your eyes at the end of the night says, "I'm tired." If you're a parent, or you've been around young children, you don't have to ask them if they're tired when they do this—you just get ready to tuck them in. In real life, affect gestures are more or less spontaneous, and are not a part of Delsarte's method. As for Cicero and Quintilian, if they cared about affect gestures at all, it was from the perspective of making sure their students did not bring them into their orative style. Did Roman audiences really want to watch a senator scratch his chest every time he adjusted his toga?

Staying with this thought, what if you could reverse the script that says our bodies are a showcase of our emotions, feelings, and moods? As performers, can the opposite be true? Of course! And this is perhaps the true gift of bringing affect gestures into our performances. One way to begin this work is through mimicry and imitation, which we've been doing our entire lives.

Desmond Morris reminds us that our self-touch, affect gestures "are unconsciously mimed acts of being touched by someone else."[17] Most, if not all, affect gestures, are unconscious, except when an actor consciously uses them to display the state of a character. When doing so, the audience sees the affect gestures as being related to the character's subconscious, even if the actor rehearsed them. Even better for the actor, when you're conscious of your affect gestures, it adds to the way that people see and receive your character. For example:

- Incorporate a handkerchief or tissue for your character, and constantly dab at your runny nose.
- Clench your left fist whenever you think about work.
- Slump your shoulders every time you hear a specific word or phrase, or when a certain character appears or speaks.

---

17 Morris, *Manwatching*, 102.

- Incorporate a nervous laugh at the mention of your mother.

This is the realm where professional speakers or politicians may hang out, eliminating these gestures as a way to control their public persona. If you are going to be giving a talk in front of hundreds or thousands of people, you may want tools and techniques to help you control your affect gestures. Conversely, an actor does the opposite: adding affect gestures as a way to augment a character's personality.

When we speak, whether as characters or in real life, our gestures fill the space in front of us, and convey meaning that our words cannot. These are new concepts for the modern actor. Affect gestures related to performance are often the result of intense imaginative exercises. The fact is, in real life, our hands do a ton of work when we're in performance. This includes filling in meaning around what we're saying.

A Shift in Perspective and Performance

Affect gestures provide actors with opportunities that other performance genres (such as opera and dance) ignore. Still, not many people in American theatre training discuss the gestures, even when most theatre exercises result in combinations that use gestures to express states of being, emotion, and action. It's important, because knowing about gestures can help an actor interpret a script beyond being written words on a page. In fact, most American theatre education remains focused on the influence of Stanislavsky's earlier methods: breaking down a role into objectives and actions and using memory or imagination to build character.

Affect gestures accompany things like action and dialog. In performance, affect gestures provide an opportunity for audience members to begin to "read" underneath your character's words—to follow along when your character is uncomfortable, nervous, or not necessarily in control. Within the psycho-physical reality of the performance, it's a chance for you to lose yourself a little, step away from your own rhythms, and embody those of your characters.

In real life and onstage, we use our bodies and our gestures to communicate before, on top of, and after our words. Modern, realism-based theatre teaching continues to emphasize our psycho-emotional states. This isn't a critique by any means, but it does make it more difficult for a performer's body to come alive on stage or screen if the corporeal instrument is rarely discussed. When your body is alive—when you are truly embodied in the performance— you convey so much more information than when you are simply emoting. In this physical performance dynamic, your body becomes a vessel through which you convey information in clearer, more powerful ways. The same is true for non-actors. When your body is alive in a meeting, or during a presentation, or on a video call, you too are more empowered in your physical communication.

Affect gestures help you shift toward this perspective, letting the body take the lead from time to time. By practicing the gesture types we've explored thus far, as well as beats (coming in Chapter 6), we can do just that.

Chapter 5 Reflections

We discover the world through our bodies. All our logic and reasoning becomes spatially oriented because that's how we understand the world. And gestures communicate what we've discovered along the way.

When we communicate, our words come out of our mouths, while our bodies actively transfer ideas and concepts our words gather into images. This means that our bodies are megaphones for our ideas—physical complements to our verbal or emotional content. When we are not talking, our bodies are still active, contributing readable messages. As we actively go about our lives, we interrupt our communication with various affect gestures that tend to the needs of the body, keeping busy in one action or another.

We constantly send physical messages through our gestures. Sometimes, such as when using emblematic gestures, our physical communication is pinpoint and direct. Other times, as with affect gestures, our communication happens seemingly behind the scenes. (Even when affect gestures are subtle, they're still communicating something to our audiences.) Meanwhile, through the way we illustrate stories with iconics, or analyze feelings and beliefs with metaphoric gestures, we share information that's highly visual and readable.

Onstage, the emblematic and affect gestures you use provide information about your character and offer new ways for your character to communicate without speaking. We can include these gestures in a realistic performance in order to bring characters to life. After all, as real people in real-life situations, we constantly touch ourselves: our cheeks, noses, and chins when we're talking; our arms as we tug on our shirt sleeves; our thighs as we slap a gesture to a close. As performers, we can lean into these types of subconscious mannerisms, make certain gestures become more specific, and bring characters to life in new ways.

In real life, most affect gestures happen subconsciously. However, when an actor brings affect gestures into a performance, the gestures become a conscious act. The audience will recognize them as being the character's unconscious movements: how they cross their arms when they talk, stand, and a host of other nonverbal cues that suggest mood, mind, or internal state of being.

By now, we have almost completed a full loop through the gesture types, starting from our earliest deictic gestures, through the landscape of iconic, metaphoric, and emblematic, then walking the realism tightrope in relation to affect gestures. Our last stop in part II will take us through improvisation and delve into beats—gestures that help form, break, and consciously reshape patterns of communication.

CHAPTER 6

Making Our Gestures Matter

It's true that many of the gestures seem to happen automatically for us, as a natural part of our speaking or communication patterns. However, as I've discussed, we can bring intentionality into the way we use the gestures and gesture types. One of the places where we see this at work is in the way we use beats as part of everyday speech. In Chapter 6, we'll take a closer look at beats, the types of co-speech gestures that many of us use all the time when we're speaking.

Beats

The beats are the gesture type that people use the most, which makes a lot of sense when you consider that most of our gestures happen when we talk. We use beats quite a bit when we're giving a speech, arguing, or trying to drive home an important point. In fact, they make up the bulk of the gestures we use in conversations. They show up often in political debates, or when someone is giving a talk, or trying to convey an important concept. As physical gesture types go, beats are straight and direct, and quite strict in their physical execution:

- One way that beats are different from other gesture types is that they typically keep the same form, no matter what the content is.

- Beats unfold in two movements (or biphasic, consisting of only the preparation and retraction), as opposed to the three-movement structure that other gesture types follow (prep-stroke-retraction). Your hand moves up and down, or in and out through the air, sometimes landing in the crest of your other hand.

- Beats do not occur in a "special gesture space." In other words, when people use beats while talking, the gesture

MAKING OUR GESTURES MATTER

tends to happen wherever the hand or hands find themselves. That might even be in a resting position.

McNeill refers to beats as "the least elaborate of gestures."[18] These flicks of the hand (or both hands) go either up or down, or back and forth, seemingly "beating" the time as part of the rhythm of speech. Even though beats don't possess discernible meaning, they tend to land on important words or sounds that correspond with the message a speaker wishes to convey. In fact, the pattern of beats emphasizes the rhythms and sounds of your spoken words. In that way, they work as tools to accentuate the urgency of the message you're sharing.

I want to come back to the last bullet above, how beats do not emanate from a special gesture space (for instance, the body's center frame or zone). The nature of beats tends to make them appear as if they're just sort of happening while a person talks, as if the hands are striking down on the words, following their own sense of rhythm. Desmond Morris suggests that people who use beats may be "only half-conscious of these moments."[19] We know that our hands are moving, but it would be difficult to provide an exact description of the movements themselves. On the surface, you might even be tempted to batch beats into the

---

18 McNeill, Gesture and Thought, 40.
19 Morris, *Manwatching*, 56.

affect gesture category. After all, in plenty of cases, speakers who use beat gestures may come across as flailing their hands around as they talk.

What Beats Say about Us (or Our Characters)

Quite often, our personalities reflect the rhythms and patterns we fall into on a normal basis, and vice versa. Think of this as our base metronome. Using beats naturally while we speak can establish a base rhythm point that we use to increase or decrease frequency. In turn, this change immediately affects the overall mood or timing of a conversation. Likewise, we can increase and decrease energy and intensity, which can immediately affect the interpretation or importance of a speech. Using beats when we speak can help reflect or amplify this reality.

Thinking in terms of political debates, or even recognizable speakers, it's fair to say that some politicians use specific beat-hand positions while speaking, in an effort to keep their physical message clean. If someone holds a hand in only one shape, it won't do much else, or distract from their message. In that way, a speaker can control or accentuate charisma by beating key words. Many performers use beats during the initial phases of memorizing a script. This can help key the right words or phrases in order to simplify complex thoughts, such as learning Shakespeare, or reciting a poem from memory, or delivering a long, rhetorical speech.

Beats are also about forming body patterns. As we embody different gestures, we discover how to magnify and maximize various movements to the benefit of how we communicate. For instance, instead of beating with the hand(s), try beating with your foot or elbow. If you beat your whole body (for instance, whenever you say the word "what") it can look like a comedic body take or reaction.

We can explore beats, as well as all gesture types, via the fact that it's within our range to shift between different character or persona types at different times during a conversation. In that way, delving into improvisation is a path that allows us to focus on ways in which we can sync up gesture types with what we're saying, and the messages we wish to convey—regardless of who we're playing, or what stage we're on.

Improv and the Embodied Performer

Improv is an area in which we can explore the many dynamics that exist across the spectrum of gestures, as well as the various effects we bring to the gestures in order to create compelling scenes: speed, repetition, and even the size of the gesture space help to serve our characters. One way to explore this begins by noticing the speed, repetition, and size of another character's gestures, then using the opposite qualities. Immediately, two very different characters appear, and a type of conflict emerges, just by choosing to invert the gesture dynamics. One easy place we see this comes across in our postures.

Posture

Sometimes we mirror individuals through matching their posture or oppose them by choosing a lower or higher posture. In improv, this leads to quick decisions that can create fun situations and scenarios (which is what improv is all about—following a "Yes, and…" track of mind means receiving the world with a playful wonder).

With every movement we enact, we carry our posture with us. You can go so far as to say that we have an innate posture that is, simply, *us*: the way we walk, stand, sit, etc. As a child, a parent or teacher may have told you to "sit up straight" in the chair, or "stand tall" in order to look confident. You may have heard words like "poised," "presence," "slouchy," etc., again and again, whether directed toward you or someone else.

In real life, posture often reflects how we feel inside. You may naturally slump when you're sad or stand broad-shouldered when you're full of confidence. On the other hand, the posture you carry around might simply be a result of bone structure, or the habitual way you've carried yourself since childhood. Just because you have rounded shoulders or a slight stoop doesn't mean you're sad—it just means that you've grown that way.

No matter what your habitual or natural posture is, if we know you well enough, we see this as your baseline, and we notice you're sad because you slump from that baseline (which may already appear "slumped"). Moving up or down from a baseline posture is how we read your body language.

Here's another way to think about a posture in relation to how we embody characters: our posture can suggest an internal or emotional disposition, regardless of how we actually feel at a certain time. For instance, if we enter a scene and are slumped over, saying, "Honey, I'm home," the audience keys in on a recognizable feature. If the character continues to operate from that posture, then we may even start to recognize people we know in real life as being familiar to the character on stage or screen.

Think back to the mirror exercise from the end of chapter 4, where we focused on body posture. The idea of that exercise was to articulate different parts of your body, down to the nuances of how your joints work and move. Consider standing, sitting, walking, or moving in a way that suggests any of the following:

- Happiness
- Confidence
- Sadness
- Defeat
- Anger
- Love

As we explore postures, we start to see links between how we carry ourselves and the effect it has on our gestures. These combinations suggest a number of personas we can adopt as performers. To that end, when we combine all the gesture types together, it's easy for us to get lost in the jumble of how to use them all. I'd like to shift focus toward three performance types that can help us understand the ways gesture types relate to each other: character, charisma, and chameleon.

A Look at Three Performance Types

First, let me offer a disclaimer: the way we view the meaning of words "character," "charisma," and "chameleon" in the real world doesn't necessarily align with my meaning here. For instance, we may strive to be charismatic in real life, but how does charisma translate onstage, in a job interview, or at the front of a room during a presentation? Likewise, to be referred to as "a real character" in the real world may not always be a positive thing, but again, the meaning for performance is different.

It may be tempting to think of these in a hierarchical sense, as if we want to "aspire" toward charisma. That's not the case. Instead, I'm using these three performance types as a shorthand categorization tool, to help sort through a number of overlapping relationships between gesture types and how we use them in performances. Rather than look at them through an aspirational lens, I'll review their underpinnings and relationships specific to their use. In that way, you can think of them as containers that hold various gestures that fit their purpose.

As communicators we tend to be creatures of habit and often revert to default gestures. Another way to say this is that each of us has our own idiosyncratic gesture style, a natural default we tend to lean into as communicators. If you're a performer, this is a great thought to carry in your back pocket when you're thinking about creating a character. If you're not a performer, this is something to think about as you begin to reflect on your own communication style.

Character

The character performance type refers to how you establish rhythms, whether fast or slow, scattered or consistent, strict or loose beats. Your posture, your voice, in fact, everything you do points back to the character you are taking on and can be constructed into a pattern or rhythm. We can think of any number of stock character types to help illustrate the character motif. For instance:

- Romantic lead
- Jealous rival
- Parent
- Bully

There are plenty of character archetypes from the world of myth or fairy tales from which we can draw, including:

- Eternal child
- Wise elder
- Trickster
- Protector

The character performance type helps to pull people into the array of idiosyncrasies you pour into your character—any number of chances with which you can spur curiosity and interest. This performance type invokes a desire to know more with attributes that grab an audience's attention and keep people focused and engaged. From that standpoint, you can lean into any number of gesture types in order to add idiosyncrasies. For instance:

- Each time you exit a scene, you give a unique wave with your fingers.

- While thinking, your fingertips play off the thumb or the chin. Every time you get something wrong, you open-palm slap your forehead with an iteration of a very personal "D'uh!"

- You push up your glasses or toss your hair often. These examples represent affect gestures.

- You are always rotating the ring on your finger. (Also an affect gesture.)

MAKING OUR GESTURES MATTER

- Your gestures may have a similar speed or location within the body zones. You always gesture from your middle zone, or next to the head, etc. Whether you're trying to create cohesion or tension, this can lead to a repeatable and expected pattern. In the end, repetitions and patterns become informative for your audience.

- You're someone who talks with their hands much more than the average person does.

- You have the tendency to mime something you're asking for (using actions, or verbs, to show the noun). For instance, "Can you bring me a mug?" (You move an imaginary mug to your lips.)

Within the character performance type, sometimes we want to offer a quick character identifier through the gesture:

- Tossing the head side to side on "I don't know!"
- Bending the ear on "What was that, Sonny?"
- Twisting your mustache while saying, "Well, isn't that interesting."

These types of gestural quirks create a basis for quickly understanding or recognizing a character—they become a snapshot of something the audience comes to expect. They can even fall into the realm of being emblematic, as they may be culturally understood. Within the character performance type, you may also find yourself leaning into certain patterns or rhythms. For instance:

- Pausing a moment before you speak, as if you're settling an idea into your body, then gesturing.
- Using all your gestures at the end of your spoken line.
- Repeating the same gesture at the start of every sentence you speak.
- Making all your gestures circular, or angular, or spiral (or a set combination of all three).
- You always lead with deictics first (just the eyes), then you move your body, then you gesture (Delsarte's succession).
- You establish a base rhythm: constantly sluggish; high-strung; etc.

Typically, transforming into a character involves breaking away from your own innate physical and verbal rhythms, and adopting new ones.

- When you're talking in character, what are you doing with your hands? Is it similar to what you do with your hands in real life? When you move away from your innate patterns, you move closer to what's real for your character.

MAKING OUR GESTURES MATTER

- When you become aware of your own gestures, it can be exciting to find another character with just a simple adjustment.

Connecting back to beats for a moment, they help to give details about the character, and can also help set rhythms for jokes. For example:

- Using beats to emphasize the wrong words.
- Chopping through the air as you talk in an exaggerated way.
- Adding a lot of flair to your beat movements as you talk by making movements with your whole arm, as if you are hacking at your own words.
- Instead of beating words with your hands, use a head nod or foot stomp instead.

Similarly, intentionally using affect gestures can create an added dimension that helps your audience see the unspoken qualities of the persona you're creating. For instance:

- You are always picking or biting your fingers.
- You dart your eyes back and forth constantly.
- You clear your throat or cough while you speak.
- You're easily startled by small noises.

These and other affect gestures create a gesture base that leads to more details about your character.

Charisma

The charisma performance type hinges on slowing down your rhythm and making seemingly deliberate movements. It evokes a sense of leadership and calm and can induce a desire to listen. The sum of your performance style—posture, gait, mannerisms, tone, etc.—is about making sure that your audience understands, feels, and sees that you're in control. More than anything, you want to pull people into your message.

In real life, we may view a charismatic person as being stoic and still, someone who commands our respect and attention. When we think about charisma, whether in a real person who possesses and emotes it, or in a character on screen, we often consider it to be a natural state, as if that person is just "born with it." The truth is, it's hard for anyone to be charismatic all the time. It requires a command of emotions and a relaxed state of stillness. The body must match the gestures, which in turn match the voice, and so on.

- With the charismatic performance type, there's seemingly no tension, nor push and pull between parts of the body. What you're saying, and how you're saying it, are in sync, and you are in control of the information you're presenting.

- Statues often embody charisma, as do classical paintings of historical figures (victorious military figures, royalty, etc.).

Charisma suggests a steady, controlled delivery. In this space, the gestures match the words, and there's a noted absence of random gestures happening between them.

- When you use any gesture, the gesture returns to a rest when you're finished. If it does linger in space, it does not waft around aimlessly, but clearly follows the three-stage movement of preparation, stroke, and retraction.

- Each gesture is specific, loaded, synced with words, and delivered with precision. Then, your hands return to their place on the table, or podium, or quietly by your sides. You hold your space in an intentional way.

With the charismatic performance type, you commit to your own rhythms and patterns again and again, and even show a tendency to slow them down. The patterns you adopt and use relate to setting and distinguishing key points in the narrative.

- For instance, you may discover eliminating all gestures from your speech forces you to curate a few hand movements that stand out. The rest of the time, your hands may be holding the sides of the podium, or finger tented in a triangle on the table. Former German Chancellor Angela Merkel is a good example of someone who used this gesture often during her political career.

- Conversely, affect gestures get in the way of the story you're telling, because they break the charismatic (rhythmic) spell. With this in mind, the charismatic performance type may tend to avoid affect gestures as much as possible, as a way to prevent any conflicting (or deceitful) messages.

Chameleon

In the real world, we might think of a chameleon as being someone who's constantly changing their colors, unable to stick to a fixed position. This ability to blend and disappear can be something to strive for in the world of performance, especially when you aspire to morph in and out of characters and personas at different times. And if you're a public speaker who has stage fright, you may find a work-around inspired by the idea of being a chameleon. Before you step onstage, you can consider the idea of literally transforming into the public speaker you want to be—stepping into your "public speaking persona" until you finish your presentation or speech. This type of distance can help lower any fear you may associate with public speaking. After all, many performers find it hard to be themselves, but find it easier to play other people.

Here's another way to think of the chameleon performance type: when an actor or performer adopts a number of roles in order to give as much information as possible about the story and the characters within a story. The chameleon performance type is all about transforming, metamorphosing, and reformatting yourself in order to shift away from who you are, and toward who the characters are (or want to be).

- During a performance, a chameleon doesn't commit everything to any one character, but rather to the full experience of the narrative or story. This is akin to the performance style of early Roman theatre.

- The first actors who performed as single individuals onstage were chameleons. They needed to lead audiences through the performance as they took on and dropped the roles of different characters at key moments in the narrative.

- Many comedic actors take on chameleon attributes as part of their acts, especially when they are in the midst of an extended story that involves multiple characters. A few names that come to mind include the likes of Tracey Ullman, the duo Joe Sears and Jaston Williams (*Greater Tuna*), Whoopi Goldberg, Dave Chapelle, Tyler Perry, Robin Williams, Jonathan Winters, and Louie Anderson.

- Within the chameleon performance type, you change characters through quick physical and emotive actions: gesture types, posture, facial expressions, tics, verbal intonations, etc.

- Your gestures will come from different zones of the body at different times, aligned with the character you're playing.

Since many of us present or perform in front of audiences at different times, adopting the chameleon performance type may indeed be the future of all presentations, as we seek to transform again and again.

- Changing from character to character requires breaking old rhythms and patterns and taking on new ones, often quite rapidly. Doing so is a way to literally morph from character to character as you flip in and out of different parts of a narrative. This requires a lot

MAKING OUR GESTURES MATTER

of focus, as the pacing and energy of the changes can slow the narrative down. A chameleon must energize their characters (and transitions), or else the energy of the performance lowers.

- In the chameleon performance type, you illustrate different gestures in ways that create the dynamics that bring characters to life.

- When you establish a rhythm for a character, you're also prepared to break it and move toward an opposing rhythm, in order to establish another character. If the rhythms are too close, it can be difficult for two characters to exist in the same space and body. A chameleon might oscillate between the first and second rhythms, so the audience sees more diversity and separation in the characters.

- What does the performer do if there are four or five characters? We use height, speed, and energy to divide our options. That way, multiple characters can share space within the narrative you're telling.

Oddly enough, while the chameleon performance type may seem the most daunting, it also might be the one that aligns closest with how we actually live. Consider: are you the same self at home as you are at work? Do you act the same around friends as you do around your family? Obviously, there's quite a spectrum to these answers, but it's safe to say that most of us shift around from time to time, depending on the room we're in, the meeting we're leading, or with whom we're sharing a meal.

Chapter 6 Reflections

Beats may not be the most elaborate gesture types, but they are the most frequently used, especially when we're giving presentations or trying to drive home a critical point in a conversation. As we talk, we tend to beat for emphasis, and each successive beat will either ramble or help us build toward a climax of thought. If you're planning to use beats as part of your speaking or presentation style, building their use around small prime numbers can be a good structure to follow (in a pattern that becomes more intense with each successive beat).

We are constantly working our way through daily rhythms and patterns. Improvisation is a tool for exploring, understanding, and learning how to accentuate or deviate from those patterns for impact and effect.

Sometimes, the patterns we create with our gestures explain specific ideas and concepts; other times, we build patterns up to create a recognized type or character. In the end, we can change our unconscious patterns and take advantage of our conscious patterns. As we do, we become integrated with those parts of our embodied performances.

- As we learn to embody different gestures, we actually discover how to magnify and maximize each movement to the benefit of our communication.

- We use beats while we're talking, telling stories, or trying to drive home a point.

At different times, we can accentuate, amplify, or even dampen our movements for effect. This understanding provides a great way to be in control of what we do, how we do it, and when we do it.

In addition, three different performance types—character, charisma, and chameleon—begin to rise to the surface as we think about the ways we take on and embody the gestures for different needs.

- Exploring the character persona is an opportunity to follow patterns that utilize certain rhythms in a way that explains a familiar character. Studying the rhythms and patterns provides a look at obeying and breaking patterns for effect; repetition; rhythm; and accentuating movements so as to convey patterns and people we know and recognize.

- The charisma persona is all about relaxing into and owning your personal rhythm, by embodying our physical gestures. It's the moment in which we are truly inside of ourselves and in complete control of what we're saying, and how we're presenting our thoughts, words, and actions.

- The chameleon persona represents our highest form in the realm of performance. Reaching the chameleon persona means we recognize how the real world moves through us. Here, we are the masters of every physical decision—we move between character and charisma personas seamlessly. As a chameleon, we can play any stage and command any room.

In our next chapter, I'd like to look at a couple of scenes from cinema, then move to an alternate take on a Shakespearean classic, in order to see what happens when we pair gestures with action, and also to showcase how the gesture types correlate and commingle, both in performance and in our daily lives.

CHAPTER 7

Leaning into Character Actions and Interactions

To help frame the exercises that we'll work through in Chapter 8, I'd like to use Chapter 7 as a way to share examples from cinema plus an alternate take on a Shakespearean classic. This part of the conversation will help broaden our understanding of the following:

- The roles of speed and repetition
- The size and precision of gesture use
- Grouping patterns (stacking or sequencing various gestures)

From the Eyes to the Body: Seeing then Acting

In Chapter 3, I started our deeper conversation about the gesture types with the eyes (deictics). Let's come back to the eyes now, and pair the work they do with other physical gestures that follow in response to what the eyes see. To do so, I've chosen two scenes from cinema, both of which you can find online.

Discovering Something That Doesn't Belong

Cary Grant, in the film *Arsenic and Old Lace*, discovers a body inside of a hideaway window seat. You can find the scene pretty easily on YouTube by searching "Cary Grant discovers body in *Arsenic and Old Lace*." The entire clip is less than a minute long.[20] The sequence is a perfect example of what's possible through the work of the eyes, facial expression, and body, as Grant's character goes from double take, to triple take, then to the nervousness of having to sit with what he's just seen.

One of the most remarkable aspects of this scene is the fact that the audience knows exactly what's in the bench seat, even though we never actually see it—again, it's all attributed to Grant's acting, in addition to one small bit of dialogue.

---

20 *Arsenic and Old Lace*, "The Gentleman in the Window Seat," directed by Frank Capra (New York, NY, Warner Bros, Ltd, 1944), Youtube.

LEANING INTO CHARACTER ACTIONS AND INTERACTIONS

At first, the story of what's in the window seat exists in Grant's eyes, then in his entire body as he sits in stunned silence. He tries to whistle, stares out the window, but can't do much more than pivot and watch as two women walk into the room. His movements suggest that he's trying to understand, or at least comprehend what's happening, but he stretches his reaction out using a series of deictic takes. It's as if he's stuck in the reaction and continues to push on this stuckness in a way that creates a comedic effect.

Here's a detailed breakdown of Grant's gestures during the sequence:

- To start, Grant's character's objective is to find "something he needs." The biomechanics here are all about the physical action of opening and closing (a drawer, the settee under the window, then another drawer).

- His objective is interrupted by his own delayed reaction: there's a dead body inside the settee.

- Here, Grant's reaction becomes somewhat Delsartian. We see succession: his eyes move first, then his body turns toward the settee in a deictic point toward attention.

- From there, the biomechanics of repetition set in: he opens the settee, closes it, sits on it, then, opens, closes, and sits on it again.

- Next, he uses deictic anchors in three spots to divide the room into spaces that seem to process the journey of his original objective; in between, he gets stuck in something of a freeze-state stare.

- Suddenly, Grant tries to whistle—a new action, rather than a gesture—but he can't make a sound, so he excuses it: his eyes flutter, and Grant gives a little "push that away" gesture (metaphoric) to mark the end of that action.

- Eventually, he returns to the three deictic anchors to unite the concept. His eyes arc left-to-right: 3. the dead body; 2. murdered; 1. my poor aunts. Then he quickly reverses the deictic anchors and Grant has finally understood the situation.

Watching it, we can't help but feel his anxiety and apprehension, not to mention the irony involved—right before he opened the bench seat, he'd been talking about a scene in a play where the very same thing (the discovery of a dead body) occurs. It's a great, angsty mix of physical

LEANING INTO CHARACTER ACTIONS AND INTERACTIONS

comedy. It also plays on a bit of cognitive dissonance: if this were a real-life situation, a person would probably run out of the room.

Looking Somewhere You Shouldn't Look

Here's another example of an actor's eyes at work, from the movie *Far and Away*. Like the Cary Grant clip, this one is also less than a minute long. You can find it on YouTube by searching "*Far and Away* Nicole Kidman Tom Cruise clip."[21]

In the scene, Nicole Kidman's character removes what is essentially a modesty bowl that's been placed over the midsection of Tom Cruise's wounded character. We can imagine what Kidman's character sees, since Cruise is clearly naked. When she first walks into the room, she's apprehensive. After a moment, she peeks under the bowl, stares, then gently sets the bowl down. Another second passes, and she smiles. Her entire posture changes. She goes for a second look. At this point, Cruise's character opens his eyes, and Kidman's character, embarrassed, hastily sets the bowl down, then flashes Cruise a shocked look. This piece of physical acting is filled with a mix of shame, guilt, and surprise.

Here's a closer look at Kidman's gestures during the sequence:

---

21 *Far and Away*, directed by Ron Howard (Universal Pictures, Los Angeles, CA, 1992), Youtube.

- At first, Kidman's character seems intent on checking in on Cruise's wounded character. However, her objective quickly changes: she wants to take a look at what's underneath the "modesty bowl."

- Before she does, she suspends her actions and establishes three deictics within the hesitation. The camera then establishes her attention at the bowl itself.

- As she approaches, she follows with two more deictics: a series of three up and down glances; and a quick side glance to make sure Cruise's character is still unconscious.

- From here she moves back into action (begins to lift the bowl). As she glances, a series of blinks work to mark the phases of her stealing a peek under the bowl. Here, her eyes stay still, which is in opposition to her nervous up and down glances from a few seconds earlier.

- Here her reaction also has a (slight) delay - first another quick side glance to Cruise before she reacts with a small right-to-left arc of the eyes.

- Next, she retracts (another action). However, this leads to a sense of temptation on her face: she wants a second look.

LEANING INTO CHARACTER ACTIONS AND INTERACTIONS

- She repeats the same biomechanical process from a moment ago, but this time a little quicker. She also repeats the three deictic anchors she's established.

- She is about to complete the whole process when Cruise begins to stir. (Had she looked left again, in a small right-to-left arc, she would have completed the whole biomechanical cycle twice.)

In both examples, the rhythm changes mid-scene. Grant's first glance into the bench seat is almost accidental—he's just walking in, completely unaware. After he looks into the hideaway bench, he casually closes it as if his brain hasn't registered what he's seen. A new rhythm emerges with his reaction. He quickly flips the lid, stares, and slams it shut. A sense of agitation takes over his body. He begins looking around the room: sitting, standing, then sitting again. Befuddled, he stares out the window, pivots to stare at the door, then into space, then at the door again. The anxiety is palpable, and it's all happening through deictic and body changes. He may have walked into the room charismatically, but by the time the two women reenter, he's gone through a complete character shift.

Kidman's character is nervous about what she's about to do. She's never seen a naked man before. When she sees what's under the bowl, her face suggests stunned silence. After she sets the bowl down, a grin breaks out. She got away with it, so why not go in for another round? To show the start of this new action, the pattern doesn't change—the rhythm does. When she goes for a second look, she isn't slow about it—she almost seems a little brash. When Cruise stirs, she acquiesces, and shoots him a glance that conveys a tumult of emotions within the span of a second or two.

These examples also give way to an important fact about the gesture types: they blend, merge, and weave in and out of each other all the time. We rarely stand around just doing deictic gestures all the time. Instead, our eyes measure the distance between here and there while our hands move through an emblematic gesture, then follow with a beat, then fold into a metaphoric gesture, then back to a beat. Meanwhile, other movements and physical messages come across via our postures. At the end of the day, we are walking dictionaries of physical messages, constantly communicating without saying a word.

Romeo Walks into a Party

What follows is another example to help illustrate the point of gestures happening in patterns and succession. I've chosen the characters Romeo and Juliet to play our leads. In the narrative, many of the same things that happen in *Arsenic and Old Lace* and *Far and Away* happen as well: a first glance; an accidental discovery; a new reality.

LEANING INTO CHARACTER ACTIONS AND INTERACTIONS

Let's start at Juliet's house. She's a Capulet, and Romeo is a Montague. None of that actually matters just yet, though the reality of their family names hangs in the air. This is their first meeting, and it's completely accidental. In fact, in this rendering, Romeo is dating someone else. He sort of ends up at this party with his friend Tybalt and a few others. He and Tybalt are carrying on a conversation as they walk into the room. That's when Romeo spots Juliet for the first time, and his life changes forever.

Romeo's first physical reaction is an affect gesture. He's nervous. When he sees Juliet, he can't help but scratch the back of his neck. He looks, looks away, then looks again—a classic double take. We're still dealing with an affect gesture, as the double take is essentially unconscious. Her beauty isn't quite registering yet, but it's starting to. He's a little stunned.

Juliet, who's talking to her cousin at the table, sees him, and for a second their eyes lock. Now Romeo is really focused, and she's focused on him as well. Then she looks away, glances back quickly, then turns away again. Watching this scene, we might be getting all the information we need just by the way they look at one another—their nervousness, discomfort, the inability to remove themselves, etc.

Then things begin to shift. Romeo's brain kicks online, and his conscious thoughts begin to pair with what he's feeling unconsciously. His posture changes. We see a slight puffing of his chest, and his body shifts to his back leg as he rounds his shoulders. It's confidence, though not swagger—he knows this young woman has noticed him, and he wants her to keep noticing. Briefly, he strikes an almost Delsartian pose—completely metaphoric, a type of stance that looks "relaxed," but not in a braggart way. It's as kind as it is confident, an emotional response but with a subtle level of conscious consideration. Juliet laughs. As the audience, we're thinking to ourselves, "He's taking on a full-body gesture that makes it look like he's in love. More than an emotion, it's an epiphany." We can almost feel Romeo's heart beating through his chest.

Now Romeo catches himself a bit. This isn't his crowd, after all. He has no idea who this girl is. He's like a ship that rights itself—he literally shifts on his feet, his eyes darting around the room. Then, noticing that no one else is looking at him, except Juliet, he sneaks another long look at her, smiles politely, and nods his head. It's a clear emblem: "*hello*" without words. Juliet smiles back, then imitates his nod. Romeo laughs.

To a degree, this is a conversation with which we're all familiar. Using these two classic characters as an example, it's almost impossible for us not to visualize the scene—it doesn't matter if we've seen the play or watched the movie. These archetypes are baked into our consciousness—teenagers falling in love at first sight. When we see Romeo's chest lift, we understand the message. There's a fluttering to what he feels, and we feel it too. It's not a codification to say we

LEANING INTO CHARACTER ACTIONS AND INTERACTIONS

understand it, exactly. It's somewhat universal, but there's another statement happening underneath. He's still looking around because he's nervous and doesn't want to get caught. Then he slowly looks to Juliet again—the girl he's destined to be with.

What does Romeo see or think when he takes a moment to consider her reaction? Maybe she's embarrassed about the whole thing, and she starts picking at her fingernails. Maybe she doesn't like the way he's looking at her, so she sticks out her chin and crosses her arms. Let's stay with the idea that she is embarrassed. Juliet's wondering, "Why is this stranger staring at me? Doesn't he know he's going to get us both in trouble?" She quickly looks away. But then she slowly looks back.

What does this look tell the audience? Remember, we still haven't heard a word of dialogue, nor seen any hand gestures. Everything is taking place with the eyes, as well as a collection of gestures at the level of posture—affect mainly, with a touch of metaphoric postures.

Assuming the actors continue to build this scene via their physical actions and reactions, then us in the audience are set to feel the entire swell of emotions: the rises and falls; the nervousness and uncertainty; the excitement and doubt, all of it coming down to physical communication.

Do you buy the idea that these two people are falling in love? If not, then what else would you need to see in this scene? Obviously, just by naming them Romeo and Juliet, and by putting them in this setting, I've borrowed a well-known scenario. Without the historical context of Shakespeare's play, are they still embodying their performances to the point where we recognize what's happening, and can see what's going on between them?

Before you answer that question, let's stay with these characters a bit longer, because things are about to change. Love is in the air. As audience members, we see and feel it in a palpable sense. Romeo starts to walk toward her, but Juliet isn't having it—not here at least. She opens her hand at the clavicle and slowly pushes it down while closing it. Here, it's our first direct metaphoric gesture with the hand that indicates to close; to lessen; to lower his impulse. Holding the end of her gesture, Juliet scans the room, then re-meets Romeo's gaze. The deeper message: caution, people are watching. She's effectively telling Romeo to temper his enthusiasm.

Still, that's not the end of the conversation. She's interested, she's just not willing to get caught up in things with her family gathered around. She glances at Romeo—a conversation of the eyes blinking—then steals a quick look at someone else, an older gentleman who's standing proud in the corner. She glances back at Romeo and nods her head twice toward the older gentleman. She's drawing a link between the two of them and this third person. It's a warning, and she's showing Romeo that this person is an issue. Her entire body changes when she glances at this man—deflation. Juliet even begins

LEANING INTO CHARACTER ACTIONS AND INTERACTIONS

to pantomime the person. He's brutish, and she puffs out her cheeks and wags her finger a bit to mimic him. Now Romeo knows exactly who she's referring to. It's a poignant imitation. Whoever that man is, friendly or not, he wouldn't like Romeo. She needs Romeo to take it easy, as this isn't the time or place to make eyes at one another.

Embodied Performances

If Romeo were a real person, or if this was happening in real life, many of his responses would fall into the category of subconscious behavior. But for an actor who is embodied in the character, we rehearse subconscious reactions or behaviors. We have acting, and our job is to lean into the performance in a way that feels real to the audience. That's where any number of physical aspects and affect responses come into play.

Even if you understand the emotional weight that Romeo and Juliet are carrying around, when you trust your physical actions, you can let them guide you through sequences and scenes. You can, in effect, propel yourself forward on the strength of your physical acting.

I've mentioned this a few times, but it's worth noting again that in the States, theatre training focuses almost exclusively on realism, and therefore the emotions. Working from this angle puts the onus on our emotions to guide us into our physical actions and reactions. Also, when you look at the broader picture of theatre arts, there are many other styles of performance that extend beyond realism: improvisation, musicals, puppetry, and plenty of others come readily to mind.

The Gesture Types and Storytelling

A variety of gesture types show up in the midst of storytelling. One place where we often find ourselves embodying characters is when we relay stories, especially when sharing stories with children. When you're telling a fairytale, you might impersonate aspects of characters in order to create an effect. A witch's cackle, for instance, is a classic voice to embody when you're telling a spooky story to a child.

To go a step further, you might stand up and take on a witch's posture—maybe you stretch your fingers out like claws, or you hunch a bit like you're brooding over a crystal ball or a vat of potion. When you step into the physicality of a witch as part of the act of storytelling, you're employing the types of techniques I shared earlier when I discussed the performance types. You're relaying a ton of information right then and there, often with a mix of metaphoric and iconic gestures.

Many comedians use this technique when they share bits with audiences. They bring a sense of physical action into these moments or set up various situations as part of their standup in order to illustrate specific moments or elements

LEANING INTO CHARACTER ACTIONS AND INTERACTIONS

in their stories. They walk us through neighborhoods, drive in the back of a car as the window goes down, use the microphone as a stand-in for some other object, all the while embodying different characters as part of their act. It doesn't matter if their stories are real or completely made up—we go there with them on the strength of their gesture types.

Performers may apply any number of gestural techniques in order to bring us into their characters, and therefore their stories: the size or scope of their gestures; a sudden body surprise or full-body reaction; an earnestness of a look. In many cases, especially for comedic purposes, it can come down to a performer's ability and willingness to circumvent expectations in order to create an unexpected reaction.

- Sometimes, the size of a response will create a specific effect. Remember our discussion of Delsarte in Chapter 4, and his assertion that the size of a gesture correlates with meaning and importance.

- An overamplification might prompt a sense of seriousness, but for comedic effect, it can also induce a sense of nervousness, anxiety, shock, or surprise. Cary Grant's reaction to finding the dead body in the bench seat is an example of conveying surprise through sudden and exaggerated bodily movements.

Many performers get stuck in the space where they want everything to come across as being authentically motivated and emotionally driven. They're forgetting that they can convey meaning through the way they handle their movements and gestures, through things like repetition, patterns—both creating and breaking them. In fact, that's a key point to keep in mind: when you establish a pattern as a character, you can use the pattern in any number of ways.

Mimicry, Impersonation, and Becoming Characters

Observing and repeating the patterns of others is a key element of mimicry and falls in line under the larger improvisation conversation. And, reflecting back to Chapter 4, there's also an overlay between mimicry and how we use iconic gestures within imitation. To extend the imitation, or move into the realm of comedy, or even absurdity, we might repeat a gesture again and again, altering the emphasis as we do, regardless of the actual gesture type.

For example, if you're going to mimic your favorite politician (or even your least favorite politician), you'll want to go farther than just getting their voice down. You'll want to hit as many elements as possible, including things like:

- Intonation and the manner of speaking
- Hand gestures
- Posture

LEANING INTO CHARACTER ACTIONS AND INTERACTIONS

- Facial mannerisms
- Verbal tics and cues
- Specific affect gestures

Hitting on their patterns again and again helps you "get in character." Plus, in the case of mimicking or impersonation, your audience often finds themselves in on the joke. They will recognize the patterns as well. In that way, you'll have easier access to pulling them into the bit, and establishing a recognizable, albeit exaggerated cadence. They won't be watching you be this person; under the spell of your impersonation, they'll be watching you "play" this person. This presents a game to the audience that is remarking on a specific feature.

Repetition

Within the realm of becoming a character, repeating a gesture is a way to establish a recognizable feature. For instance:

- Tossing your hair can add comedic flirty energy to a dialogue.
- A schoolmarm (type) standing erect at the door, slowly slapping her yardstick into her open palm, suggests an air of authority or a rigid nature.

Similarly, if you want to mimic a friend of yours, and get other friends to laugh (lightheartedly, of course), you might tease out a gesture you've all seen your mutual friend repeat over and over. This is another way to open the door into becoming this character. Again, patterns—the use, amplification, and size at different times—are keys to establishing character and persona.

Changing Patterns

Another way to approach this as a practice is to challenge yourself to change patterns. For instance, while talking, double the number of gestures you use; or limit yourself to one gesture per sentence or thought. You can even walk behind a person on the street and attempt to match their swing of arms, or the bounce, distance between, and speed of their steps. When you do, what happens to your emotional state? Your attitude? Do you see the world differently? Does your attitude shift in one way or another? How would you grade this shift in perspective?

Exaggeration

Exaggeration is another opportunity that can provoke fun in the way we hold and carry ourselves and exhibit the gestures at different times. As we saw in the Cary Grant example from earlier, you can register your reactions to situations and stimuli in gestures. Plus, the size of your gestures can exaggerate the reaction for comedic effect. Again,

LEANING INTO CHARACTER ACTIONS AND INTERACTIONS

this is related to the notion the gestures have different sizes, whether out of comedic effect, or simply because your message demands it:

- The way you match your dog's "hello energy" when you come home.
- When your boss places a stack of papers on your desk and walks away, you turn to your work colleague and pretend you're drowning.
- Laughing a little louder and longer at your own corny "dad jokes" that your teenage son thinks are lame.

Sticking with this last note, when you react to something with a little more energy than it warrants, you can produce a number of effects: irony, comedy, drama, surprise, uncertainty, intentional discomfort, etc. Subverting expectations does similar work:

- Everyone in the family celebrates the wedding announcement, but you flash a deflated, ironic victory arm, followed by an underwhelming "oh joy" about your new brother-in-law.

- The doctor says you have two weeks to live. You shrug your shoulders and say, "I want a second opinion." The doctor replies, "Okay, you're ugly, too," to which you gasp, put your hand to your mouth and exclaim, "Oh!"

Playing off different characters is another way where you can subvert expectations, and create comedy, tension, irony, drama, etc. In our Romeo and Juliet sequence, Juliet calms Romeo with a gesture of her hand. Let's pretend that Romeo didn't calm down—he was too enraptured. Now, what if she were to have done the opposite, and met his gaze with something of a challenge? For instance:

- The flirtatious tossing of the hair, which I mentioned above.
- A classic batting of the eyes while rubbing the neck with her fingers.
- Or, staying with the eyes, a deictic nod to another area of the room, as if to say, "Meet me over there."

How would things have played out in any of these scenarios? Would Romeo have moved beyond his freeze state and acted upon an invitation? In either case (the scene we created in the Romeo and Juliet scenario, or the idea of the invitation), Juliet's gesture enacts a type of control over the situation. It's almost like a silent pantomime: she meets Romeo's gaze with her reaction, to which Romeo must respond.

Chapter 7 Reflections

Whether or not we're trained performers, we can practice various aspects of the performance types I introduced in Chapter 6 and build upon some of the biomechanical work I discussed elsewhere throughout this book. We can also begin to get more out of our gestures based on some of the elements we looked at in Chapter 7, including:

- Responses and amplification
- Speed and repetition
- Grouping various patterns
- Pairing gestures with actions
- Pairing posture with gestures
- Playing off different characters

In the space of embodied performances, we can let our physical actions and reactions guide characters as they work through emotions, surprises, secrets, and any number of moments where they oscillate between fright, fight, or flight. As well, if an emotion ends in a physicality, we can repeat the physical gesture in order to return to the emotion, or vary them to show a change of state. Think back to how Cary Grant's physical response followed a series of gestures—he is responding to something he was not expecting. Meanwhile, Nicole Kidman's gestures paired with a number of movements that fall into the broader category of actions—she was making action-oriented choices as she pursued an objective. While the actions moved her forward, the gestures told us what was happening in her mind, as she went from feeling nervous and apprehensive upon her first glance under the bowl, to being a little over-confident with her second peek.

Now that we've explored the gestures with the help of characters, it's time to continue the work of building your own physical performance repertoire, complete with a series of easy exercises and practices you can do from just about anywhere.

CHAPTER 8

Building Your Practice

The six gesture types I've focused on throughout this book exist on a continuum and are constantly in conversation with one another. We've been using them our whole lives and distributing them around without knowing it. When we observe them, they do not always fall neatly into one category or another, nor do we use them in silos. Instead, they share a mutual relationship, and often fold out one after the other, spilling into and on top of one another, in a constant, steady succession of movements, motions, and patterns.

In real life, we cycle through gestures and gesture types, whether we're talking to a friend, retelling a story, or standing up to give a presentation. The same is true for performers, especially those who look for ways to make physical acting part of their performance style.

The newest research suggests our gestures indicate the brain at work. They emanate from thought, and actually provide our audience—whether it's a single person or a room full of people—a physical rendering of what we see in our mind's eye. At the same time, the act of gesturing can also help us as speakers and storytellers arrive at specific conclusions we're trying to communicate verbally. In that way, we are both sending messages to other people, and even, perhaps, conveying them for our own sake of clarity.

One of my goals in writing this book is to show how the gestures interact and correspond with each other. Another key point about the gesture types involves intentionality. In this chapter, I'd like to explore both themes, while sharing a number of exercises and practices you can turn to as you continue to put intention toward your use of the gesture types. Before I do, let's quickly review some of the ground we've covered.

Our Modern Relationship with the Historical Context

When we take a close look at the history of the gesture types, we recognize that our society continues to influence the communicative potential of our bodies. We are a culture

BUILDING YOUR PRACTICE

of content. In recent years, more and more of our attention has begun to lean in the direction of podcasts, emojis, and the tight, shoulder-up camera angles so prevalent on social media and live streaming. That's not to say that physical modalities no longer matter, because they do—just think of any number of social media dance challenges.

If there has been an ebbing of physical expression in our society, especially now, as we are all armed with cameras, then I would like to resuscitate our human nature as physical communicators. I believe that gestures can lead us back into everyday, common embodiment, and that we can do so through the lens of theatre and performance. It's not the only way through which you can renew this exploration into our historical selves, but it certainly is one avenue worth taking. In that way, I've tried my best to keep our conversation as broad as possible, and to avoid codifying a meaning that says, in effect, "Do X in order to convey Y."

Performers use spontaneous gestures in realistic theatre, even though there's an entire history of theatre that relied heavily on the body—a history that isn't all that long ago. Modern science has confirmed what actors and public speakers have practiced for millennia: that our gestures represent key links into how we communicate to others.

The change into enacting subtle movements has been fueled by our ability to bring the fourth wall (the "eye") closer to us, via our handheld cameras. It's similar to the idea of two people talking across a table: the size of gestures is appropriate for the distance. Now, if these same two people have a conversation across a parking lot, or even on opposite sides of a large room, the gestures will magnify to compensate for the distance between them. The gestures are operational no matter the distance, and science has helped uncover what we lose when we take our bodies out of the equation.

Something I've discovered in recent years is that as technology has given us new ways to connect with audiences the world over, it has also drastically reduced our communications learning curve. People aren't bothering themselves with taking theatre or performance classes before launching their live stream podcasts. In a way it's exciting, because we have access to so many opinions. Still, with so much competition for our attention, words aren't enough. If a camera is present, then the body is present under your words.

Going from Spontaneous to Intentional

We see people use spontaneous gestures in the real world all the time—at the grocery store, the bank, a neighborly conversation, with loved ones over dinner, etc. Perhaps as you've spent time with this book, you've begun to track your own spontaneous movements, or found yourself giving thought to why you're using your hands the way you do. At the end of the day, even though I've spent a lot of time talking about performers and performance, the gesture types belong to all of us. After all, we are constantly making efforts to get points across, and to share messages that matter—to be heard among the steady din of the world in which we live. Like the orators of Cicero and Quintilian's time, being louder allows us to be heard, but may not produce the effects we want. However, being seen is a different story, and an opportunity to help us reach the connection we're hoping to achieve.

So, even if most people don't spend time thinking about their gestures in advance, I believe we can all benefit from forethought, followed by a direct physical interaction as part of our normal patterns of speech.

In rehearsal, a performer might choose or lock in on a specific pattern: a way of carrying his or her shoulders or posture; an effect of the hands; some curated gestures, etc. From that perspective, my hope is that this book proves to be extremely helpful as you find new approaches to expand, enhance, or refine the physical aspects of your performances.

For non-performers, I hope the same. Business education will often center physical training on public speaking skills. However, we continue to use gestures in office meetings, around the water cooler, and in any number of non-performative, one-on-one moments. Understanding and practicing the gesture types in this book will help facilitate the way you use them and deepen your experience of what you're doing with your body when you're talking, presenting, or sharing information.

YOUR VISUAL CONNECTION

In the end, it doesn't matter if you're trying to command a room, or gain traction on social media; if you're a semi-professional, amateur, or a seasoned performer; if you work in an office, or are running for office: if you feel like something's missing in your performance style, but you don't know what it is, I hope that this book has been both a guide and a platform to go deeper into your understanding of the six gesture types.

Start with the Eyes

In puppetry and biomechanics, the eyes equal attention. Deictics involve the act of pointing at nouns, while puppets come alive when their heads move, and their eyes move along with them. Even if nothing else moves, just the head and the eyes are enough to evoke a sense of life and aliveness. From this state, when you, a puppet, or even a baby looks at something, and then repeats the glance, that thing, whatever it is, gains more meaning and importance. During a performance, our eyes create attention that others follow. We can set other things in spaces—characters, objects, essentially any other noun—simply by using our eyes, and can amplify this to varying degrees with the addition of the body: opening our stance; lengthening the torso; opening the arms, etc.

Moving along this thread, biomechanics are all about the body and our movements. Following that, we talked quite a bit about Delsarte, and how our gestures work in various spaces, typically emanating from various frames or zones of the body. Pairing biomechanics with Delsarte, deictics of the hands and eyes move in sync with one another in order to create an additional effect. Conversely, if they move in opposition of each other, this will also create an effect, sometimes comedic, or filled with aspects of tension, agitation, uncertainty, etc. Staying with this Delsarte dynamic, his discourse invites us to organize other parts of our bodies in concert with the eyes: the head, fingers, torso, chest, arms and so forth. As we create and follow this flow, we do so with a sense of harmony.

Movements within Movements

Within the conversation about biomechanics, there's also the notion of growth cycles, and how much work they can do for a performer. For example, you may show an emotion on the face, while the corresponding movements of the body can make the emotion bigger or smaller. This becomes a bridge to mime and pantomime. You can take the idea of "happiness" and start to reveal it through widening your eyes. Then, you can expand the idea through your smile, or raising your eyebrows. But you're not done. Now, you can bring your body into the idea. Your head tilts back, your eyes track upwards like you're following a balloon lifting into the air; your chest opens; your arms extend; your fingers stretch as far apart as possible. It's not only that you're happy—now you look like a

YOUR VISUAL CONNECTION

giant sunflower starting to open. Indeed, your entire body is smiling. From there, if you were to unwind the gesture and return to your previous state, you might be inclined to do so in reverse: tighten the span of your fingers; bring your arms back in so they're closer to your body; fix your gaze straight ahead (no longer tracking something above) until you arrive back at the smiling eyes that kicked the entire thing off.

When we start to talk about metaphorical and iconic gesture types, we often find them affecting posture and attitudes of the body. From there, we enter into the world of miming, impersonation, and imitation. Many of these elements date back to ancient Roman theatre, where solitary performers took on aspects of different characters in order to bring their audiences into their stories. Today, we see similar notions play out among standup comedians and one-person storytellers, including those who make impersonations part of their routines. In the end, the idea remains the same: to bring audiences into the action.

To do so, these performers rely on a mix of iconic and metaphoric gestures that put known objects into space (iconic) and exemplify a range of emotions and abstract thoughts (metaphoric). When you spend time in this space, you discover that you can imitate just about anything around you, and even create a spectrum of characters out of thin air.

To adopt a character from within a story—more precisely, to adopt characteristics so as to embody a character—pushes this notion even farther. You effectively begin to display various details of the narrative from the persona of that character. In many ways, this mixes nearly every aspect I've touched upon to this point and serves as an ideal bridge into our final exercise.

From Inside the Story

Quite often, when we see people use iconic or metaphoric gestures, it's in the act of telling a story. I mentioned above that many modern comedians rely on a mix of iconic and metaphoric gestures in order to bring audiences closer to the action. When they do, they effectively become another character, even if for only a few seconds at a time: the way a character stands, walks, points to another character, expresses an idea, or performs any number of actions, etc. As they become this person, the story takes on a new dimension. As a member of the audience, we're no longer just watching a comedian tell a story—we're transported into the story, and that much closer to the experience.

David McNeill points this out when he discusses spontaneous gestures. Many of us, when we tell stories, intuitively use iconic gestures as part of the telling, whether we are trying to exemplify physical objects that exist in the story, or take on an aspect of a certain character. A witness to this type of storytelling is akin to seeing inside the storyteller's brain: we see the object as they see it in their mind's eye. Meanwhile, the storyteller is giving audience members as close a glimpse into their thoughts as possible.

The physical gesture types that occur beneath our language detail key points of the narrative we share, and demonstrate the things that we find important in the telling—the witch's crooked finger, for instance; the hero's posture with arms akimbo, head in profile; the trusty sidekick fidgeting in the face of danger. In the moment of storytelling, gestures illustrate the elements of a story that we find most important, often through embodying characters. In that way, the gestures help to create a richer and more lasting sense of story craft.

As an actor, tapping into the physical side of performance can be some of our most important work. We bring audiences deeper into the performance with every gesture we make, along with how and when we make them, how often we repeat them, the speed with which we use them, and the patterns we create and break.

We see this notion quite a bit in storytelling that's geared toward children, not just theatre and performance, but also when reading a book, or sharing a story with a child. We make things big; we slow our gestures down in order to pause time; we create suspense with sudden stops, or staring off into the distance; we induce surprise with quick, panicky movements. We may suggest slight postures with the voices we use when we retell *Goldilocks and the Three Bears*, or exemplify physical attributes of the three little pigs with our hand positioning, or exaggerate the wolf's gestures as he threatens, "I'll huff, and I'll puff, and I'll blow your house down!" If you're a parent, or someone who has worked with children, you might not even be conscious of the fact that you're doing this. These types of responses to elements in a story might just come naturally to you as an aspect of entertainment, or because you're trying to help your young listeners enjoy the experience that much more. But this type of performance—making yourself big, or frightening, or funny—creates a visual experience for listeners that rises up and out of your body, and begins to live in theirs.

This idea takes me back again to Delsarte, and the idea of conveying metaphors through postures and poses. It begs one more variation of this question: Where does honesty live in your body? How does one show virtue? Joy? Faithfulness? Can we create these metaphoric emotional states via postures? If so, in what zones or frames? My larger point here is this: as you feel and convey these messages, you also create them for your audience. In the end, you trust your body's biomechanics, and you move these metaphorical gestures outward: from a granular, internalized state, into your external storytelling.

Integral Movement in Performance Practices

Integral movement in performance practice is something I studied years ago in Berlin. In the words of Thomas Prattki, it is "personal development through movement and performance-based process work, which explores a practice for artistic individuation, self-realization, and the emergence of a more embodied consciousness."[22] I want to bring this into our conversation now as you build new ways to stay with the gesture types and incorporate them into everyday practices. Doing so is an opportunity to make your body a core piece of overall expression; to bring awareness to how you move in communication. For example:

- Being conscious of your movements, the space you occupy, and how you register the distance between yourself and the objects or people around you.
- Observing your daily physical rhythms and transformations.
- Curating your gestures (especially metaphorical) to clearly express abstract concepts, feelings, ideas, etc.
- Being aware of using your words and gestures in concert and deepening your connection to thought.
- Finding the joy of sharing your best self with others around you and seeing your interactions with neighbors and friends as fertile ground for improving the relationships that require kindness and empathy.

---

22 Thomas Prattki, "Integral Movement and Performance Practice," accessed September 30, 2017, https:www.thomasprattkicentre.com.

Usually as we're moving through our days, we come in contact with a number of different roles: consumer, parent, friend, coworker, etc. Each requires that we operate in a relationship: consumer and seller; parent and child; colleague and peer; friend and friend. Without one, the other doesn't exist, so we adopt one role and follow something of a "script," like a social contract. In owning and being aware of these roles, we gain individuality by perfecting those parts of ourselves that "show up" in various roles, performing our individuality by playing the same community role that everyone plays, but in our own (ideally better) way. This means we are aware of being seen because performance requires an audience. As we integrate ourselves into various roles, we gain ownership of our bodies—we realize ourselves as individuals.

How do we move so seamlessly from role to role, and consciously transition from one to the next? Let's keep this question in mind as we delve into our exercises.

Exercise 1: Working with Attention

This exercise focuses on deictic gestures and setting people and things in space. It's fun, and perhaps a little devious. Be sure to choose a good friend, or someone who won't think you're rude for being distracted during a video call. (Full disclosure, I like to do this toward the start of my online classes, as a way to introduce play to my students.) Consider parking this exercise as an idea for your next video call. You could even plan a call with friends or family members, and then put this exercise to work without telling them what's happening.

- During the video call, allow yourself to become distracted by something off-screen. You can do this on your end of the call, or you can do this with the person with whom you're speaking (more on this in a moment).

- While you're talking with your friend or group of friends (or family members), quickly look off to the left and gesture to an imagined person. Ask the imaginary person, "Can you please stop doing that?" Return to the call, then repeat your line, looking off to the left again. This time, add a phrase like, "Yeah, well, same to you!" Return to your call and apologize for the interruption. Can you make your friends believe there are other people in the room distracting you?

- You can challenge yourself, and change the effect, by changing the deictic direction. Instead of looking off to the left before you speak, what happens if you look up at the ceiling, or down at the floor? Are you talking to an imaginary pet now? A spider on the ceiling? A ghost?

- On your end, it can be helpful to locate an object in the room where you're sitting that you'll use as an anchor. Or, without using a specific object, you can simply fix on an area to your left or right, or above your screen's camera, or below (which works best if you're sitting at a desk), glancing away then back in patterns of three, five, and seven.

- Taking things to the next step, pretend that someone else (or something else) has entered the room, and wants your attention. You can go so far as to start with small gestures toward the person, then build into a conversation or an argument that uses bigger and bigger gestures. How do you tease out this performance? How do you use the camera frame around your body? How do you build the rhythm that splits your attention?

- Look past someone's shoulder, or at a specific spot on their shoulder while you're speaking, but not while you're listening. Now, try looking in your purse or a desk drawer. What kind of deictics do you give? Try finding a slow rhythm.

- If you pick up on the fact that they notice you keep looking, ask them, "What's that?" without being specific. Play around a little bit. Make them keep trying to figure it out.

Your friends might become annoyed if they don't know what you're doing, so let them know that you're practicing deictic gestures. (If they don't know what deictic gestures are, start by explaining how they point and place things, real or unreal, in space, and expand the world of a performance or presentation.) Here's a separate exercise that's also about attention and can help with public speaking. You can practice this in front of a group of friends, or even on a video call:

- Deliver the following line with mock importance: "I must tell you about the best thing I ate yesterday." Let your gaze pan from right to left across the room in one smooth arc.

- Now, deliver the same line again, but divide your gaze into two smaller arcs.

- Repeat the line a third time and divide your gaze across the room in thirds.

How does your arc affect the line of dialogue? Which arc felt most natural to you? Which one felt most aligned with the line of dialogue?

Exercise 2: Working Out of Sight

This exercise is similar to the previous but deserves its own subsection. Your goal is to make your friends think that you're talking to someone at the door. Here's how it goes:

- With your friends in the room with you, open the nearest door—it could be at the front or back of your house or apartment, or even a door into another room. Whatever you do, make sure your friends can't see out the door—only you have that vantage point.

- Begin a conversation with the "other person" who's at the door. You can also pretend that the other person is across the street, or across the hallway in an apartment building. Remember, your goal is to "sell" the idea that you are really talking to another person.

- As best you can, continue your animated conversation with the other person, letting your gestures do the work. As you go, oscillate between talking to the person at the door, and talking to your friends. Can you make them believe that someone is really there?

Exercise 3: Working with Zones

We spent quite a bit of time discussing Delsarte in Chapter 4. These next couple of exercises bring us back to the zones of the body, as well as themes of balance, opposition, and succession. Feel free to flip back and forth to the images I shared in Chapter 4, on the zones of the body, and Delsarte's triads. This exercise is for all three zones.

- Use a line of text (such as "You give me no choice") with each gesture.

- Stand and clasp your hands below the waist, while slightly raising your head. Speak the line.

- Next, clasp your hands tighter, then raise them to your chest. As you do, drop your head as your hands move upward. How does the line change?

- Now, clasp the hands even tighter, and drop your head as low as you can as your hands rise above the head. Be sure that your movements are happening simultaneously—keep the idea of flow in mind. Can you commit the line to this feeling of conflict?

BUILDING YOUR PRACTICE

- Ask yourself: Where are your eyes looking? Where are your feet pointing?

Here's another zonal exercise that also focuses on a gesture's three-phase structure (preparation, stroke, and retraction). The goal here is twofold: to delve into how a gesture changes as it moves through different zones, and to slow down and explore the variations that occur between the three phases. To do so, we'll use a classic "stop" sign.

- To prepare, let's find our harmonic balance. Poised with a balanced center, stand firm with your legs balancing your weight, your arms at your sides. From that position, tip your weight so your right leg is holding most of it. Incline your head to the right and ease your torso to the left. Does this stance feel familiar? Would you say you feel more or less balanced than before?

- From this position, choose one arm, and bring it to chest level; this is the preparation phase of the gesture. From there the stroke of the gesture occurs: extend your arm, while simultaneously opening your palm into the "stop" sign. This is the end of the stroke phase. Hold it there for a moment, then retract the hand and arm back to the side. When you're done, repeat the gesture with your other arm.

YOUR VISUAL CONNECTION

- Here's a variation: complete the gesture again, but this time add a spoken line: "Don't come any closer." Try it a few times, speaking the line to correspond with different phases of the gesture: speak the whole line during the preparation, or just during the retraction. Where do the words feel most powerful? In the preparation? The stroke? The retraction?

- Let's try the same sequence again, but this time from a lower zone, extending your arm and hand away from your hip rather than from your chest.

- Now again, but this time, repeat the movement from the space above your head.

- Now for another variation: repeat the line, but this time, begin the gesture at your head zone and end the stroke of the gesture in your torso zone (essentially moving through zones). Does this diagonal movement lengthen the gesture or the spoken line?

- Repeat, once more, but start the stroke of the gesture in the torso zone and finish it above the head. As you do, check in with yourself. What are your feet doing? Can you step forward with the gesture? Where are your deictics? Do they move in parallel or opposition with the phases of the gesture movement? What happens when you extend the gesture in a different way? Instead of straight out from the body, what happens if your arm curves to a stop? What if your arm spirals as you extend outward? How do these changes affect the speed or power of your spoken line?

What do you notice as you make these changes, and come from different zones? Is there a different velocity or veracity to your spoken line? Does your body feel more affirmative in your stance or posture? Or is there comedy at different times?

Exercise 4: Working with and against Your Thoughts

This sequence of exercises will challenge you to think in two directions. The purpose of this exercise is to explore the variations that exist between your body and gestures.

- To start, find a body position that is "up" (chest is lifted; head held high, etc.) while your face is down ("frown," "heavy eyes," etc.).

- From that position, describe the last thing you ate. As you do, notice whether your gestures follow the posture of your body, or your face.

- Now, I'd like you to invert what you're doing with your body and with your face: scrunch the body down (slouching, arms resting on the legs, etc.) while lifting the face up (looking up, smiling, eyes wide, etc.). From that position, describe your favorite meal.

- From this preposition, begin to expand the body out: open the space between elbows and torso; point your legs out; puff the chest broadly. How does this affect your gestures?

- Now, bring the body back in: pull your elbows in at the side; tighten the gap between your legs; compact the chest; etc. Does this change your breathing, too?

- What do you discover yourself thinking or feeling as you work through these movements? As you speak through these variations, do you use different words or speech tones? Does your body override the expressions on your face? Is the opposite true? Do you find yourself landing in some kind of conflict, or a balance where the body and thought or emotion eventually sync up?

Staying with this idea, what happens when you oscillate between the two? Let's work with directions (up and down; out and in).

- Hold onto the downward feeling in the body and try to rise up from that body position, without showing any movement. Now, from that state, notice the feeling that takes your body back to "down."

- Hold onto the upward feeling in the body and try to lower yourself from that body position without showing movement. Notice the adjustments you feel you make.

Here's another one that works with and against your thoughts: try putting one emotion on your face, while adopting an opposing rhythm in your body. This exercise helps you explore the limits that come up when your body is trying to convey multiple messages at once.

- For instance, how does sadness on your face play when conveying fast gestures in your body?

- What about a look of surprise on your face when using slow gestures in your body?

- What steps or movements can you take to sync these emotions up and reinforce the mood with gestures?

Finally, here's an exercise that involves the beats—aligning with and against your thoughts:

- To start, I'd like you to speak this familiar piece of text: "To be or not to be; that is the question."

- Next, I'd like you to speak it again. This time, strike down (beat) on words that in your mind are the most important. (I won't tell you which ones you should choose—it's up to you.)

- Now, let's do it again, but this time, I want you to strike (beat) on the words that are in ALL CAPS: "To be OR not TO be; that is THE quest-ION." After you run through this round of the exercise, spend a moment reflecting. What effect do these strikes produce? Do they change the way you understand the line?

- Now, let's try it again, but this time we'll follow the logic of the line. Strike on the words in ALL CAPS: "To BE or not to be; that is the QUEST-ion." What effects do these strikes have on how you speak the line? Do you fall in a rhythm? Or do the strikes seem to push back against your own natural inclination?

Exercise 5: Working with Masks

To a large degree, my personal journey through the gesture types began to come alive when I first worked with the

BUILDING YOUR PRACTICE

neutral mask. You don't even need to have a neutral mask lying around to work without using your face. You can use a brown paper bag with eye holes if you want, or stand before a mirror with only your body showing (your head out of the reflection, similar to some of the work you did in Chapter 4). However you do it, look for a way to remove your face from the work, and present the body as the main communicative device.

- Covering your face essentially puts you in a position where you have to put more emphasis on communicating with other parts of your body—your facial expressions won't be much help in this one.

- When you take the face away as a tool of expression, communicating through the body becomes more important. Many of us may have experienced this at different times during the COVID-19 pandemic, when we were all wearing masks.

- While watching a recording of yourself, you can place a hand or a card over or on the head and watch the body. However, you may be unable to make immediate changes in real time to your movements (as standing before a mirror).

- With your face covered, run your gestures through the sequences or variations of six basic emotions: sadness, happiness, surprise, fear, anger, disgust. Look for moments to oscillate, contrast, and work with your body to magnify and minimize the emotions in the body (we will see movement here).

- What do you notice about your body when you can't rely on your face to express the various thoughts and feelings? Do the biomechanics of your movements change, or are they different from when you did the same exercises without the mask? How? Why do you suppose this is the case?

Here's another mask exercise that uses suggested expressions or characters. This time, you'll use a brown paper bag. On one side of the bag, draw three large nines, or commas in a triangle (the apex pointing down). On the other side of the bag, draw three large sixes (upside-down commas) in a similar triangle. Can you see two emotions or characters?

- With the help of a mirror, choose one side of the bag, and try to get your body to match the emotion.

- Once you feel like you're getting it, switch it up, flip the bag around, and move through the opposite emotion.

What changes do you observe as you slide between these characters? Are there any overlaps? As you practice again and again, see how large you can make the distinction between your two characters. Also, notice your successions. Do your characters fold in and out of each other? Or are the changes dramatic and noticeable? (There's more on successions below.)

Even though you're covering your face, this exercise is very much about seeing yourself, which is why you'll want to have a mirror around. Short of having a mirror, you can also record and watch yourself later. The main point is that when you take your face away, the body becomes magnified to the point of taking over. Eventually, it's not the mask offering an expression, but your body.

Finally, here's a related exercise that moves into the realm of mimicry. You'll need to watch or stream a video of someone talking to a crowd. I've found that a late-night host's monologue, a motivational speaker, or a politician who's not hidden behind a podium work pretty well for this.

- After you choose the person you'll mimic and find your video, the next thing to do is to cover the upper portion of the screen so you don't see their head. Your goal is to focus on their bodily gestures.

- Next, you'll want to turn the sound all the way down. The content of what they say is less important than practicing the way they say it with their bodies.

- At the start, you may want to watch a full minute or two before you even try to mimic a gesture. Once you feel ready, rewind to the start of the video. This time, see how much you can mimic before you hit pause. You might also find that it's helpful to go a few frames at a time.

- If this seems too daunting at the start, one way to simplify your practice is to focus only on one part of their body. For instance, can you target their posture? Their hand gestures? The way they tug on their suit coat, or put their hands in their pockets between jokes?

These types of exercise bring the body into the communicative process in a dramatically new way. You'll discover that when you take the mask off, your body acts (when practicing the gesture types again) in a way that suggests it is living more completely in your movements. This is a great practice to do on a regular basis, in order to really extend the work of the body.

Exercise 6: Working with a Succession of Movements

Succession is the unfolding of a movement: where it starts and ends in the body.

Succession is a close cousin to biomechanics. It recognizes the transfer of movement through the body, and both acknowledge the start and end of a movement. In this exercise, I'd like you to focus on the succession of movements you make while you're doing fairly normal, daily activities, such as walking, standing from a chair, sitting down, or even shifting from side to side in your seat.

- Tracking your succession of movements involves focusing on nearly every part of your body. Walking includes the joints, your spine, hips, knees, ankles, but also the swing and sway of your arms from the shoulders down to the tips of your fingers.

- As you stand up from your chair, what do you do first? Do you slide your hands out to grip the armrests? Or, if you're in a chair with no armrests, how far forward do you lean before you push up from the seat? Do you look down as you rise up? When do you lift your gaze?

- When you walk down a hallway and greet someone, do you start with your gesture, then smile? Or smile, then wave hello?

- While talking with friends, your gestures most likely sync with the words you say. Can you try to gesture first, and then verbally make your point? Conversely, can you verbally share an idea before gesturing (or without gesturing at all)?

- What happens to your walking gait when you focus your thinking and movement on sending your shoulders backwards or forwards? What about when you send your right leg and your left shoulder forward (balance of walking)? Do you send your shoulder first, then take your step? Do you step first, then send your shoulder? Can you sync them up by removing succession?

This exercise can be a powerful reminder that we move through life playing different roles and are not always aware of the physical changes that we make to adopt those roles. Focus on our biomechanics with these daily movements can help us stop and appreciate the body at work.

Here's a totally different succession exercise using the deictics, focusing on takes and variations. As I wrote in Chapter 3, performers bring takes into their bits for various effects (irony, humor, surprise, etc.). In *Arsenic and Old Lace*, Cary Grant's character gets stuck in a quick succession of takes after he discovers the body in the chest drawer. Practicing takes can be pretty fun, and something you can easily bring out into the world with you. If you're not ready to practice your takes in front of people, you can do so on your own.

BUILDING YOUR PRACTICE

- To start, have a seat, and look straight ahead. Pick an object in the room from the periphery, either right or left. Turn your whole head toward it at what you'd consider to be a normal pace, glance, then turn back to center.

- Now, repeat the gesture, but quicken the pace.

- Repeat the gesture again. This time, before you bring your glance back to center, return to the object.

- Repeat the gesture again. This time, try to vary your turn. Instead of swinging your whole head to and from, then back to the object, only bring the eyes back the second time. What do you notice when you do this? Does it feel natural? Comedic? Odd? Quirky?

You can practice this gesture in a number of ways. For instance:

- Instead of returning to the object in a quick manner, you use a slow steady turn of the head (the classic "slow burn"). I have found that the slower the turn, the bigger the laugh. (When you do the slow burn, what are your deictics doing?)

- You can also use the slow burn with anchors and turn this exercise into preparation for a speech or monologue.

Exercise 7: Retelling a Fairytale

Nearly everyone appreciates a fairytale ending. While this book isn't exactly a story, the study of the gesture types can be a journey, one that is indeed never-ending. With that in mind, I want to offer a final exercise that brings many of the things we've looked at and discussed into focus and gives you a chance to move around through different characters and gesture types.

- To start, think of a favorite fairytale. Perhaps you want to refer to a book or something you can find online as a refresher. Although it can be your own story, fairytales allow us to create known characters that are familiar to us, in big, archetypal ways.

- Now, give the story a good retelling from the perspective of a third-person omniscient narrator. Or, if it's a firsthand account of a true story, or something you've created in the first-person voice, tell it from this place. Track the gestures you use at different times, paying special attention to how you verb your nouns, and how gestures express meta-narrative choices: time, feelings, changes/transformation, etc.

- In this telling, begin adding the body into various character personas when different people or things show up in the story. Maybe you're telling a shortened version of *The Wizard of Oz*: Do you mimic the movie? How do you evoke the Wicked Witch when she shows up? How about the Cowardly Lion? Tin Man? How does your posture change when you tell and retell parts of the story from varying perspectives?

What happens if you add more of the space to the story? For instance, what if your gestures all happen at arm's length (around you)? What type of tension does this create in your storytelling? Can you still make the retelling work to the effect that you're hoping for? For instance, how do you evoke fear from this one confined space? What about sorrow? Joy? Surprise?

Chapter 8 Reflections

I'd like to share one more thought as we wrap up Chapter 8: the narrative space that lives inside of a story is the space that exists around us at all times. When we lean into the six gesture types, we can do nearly anything with this space, and within this space.

- Through deictic gestures, we can expand it, direct our way through it, and apply new meaning to people and things.
- Metaphoric gestures help us create visual meaning to abstract ideas within the space.
- With iconic gestures, we can bring physical things into space.
- Emblematic gestures can help our audience feel familiar within a space.
- Via intentionally using affect gestures, we can reveal or restrict who we are (in performance space).
- Finally, with beats, we create new emphasis and rhythms on top of what's happening in the space.

When all is said and done, commanding the fourth wall is about holding people's attention. I hope that your tour through *Your Visual Connection* provides enough information, insight, and activities to gain and keep yours.

Conclusion

Everything we learn in life is based on our physicality. From this base of understanding, we begin to reason through an onslaught of ideas that come at us from every direction. Soon, we start to apply meaning onto things, and to create understanding or connections between people, places, and objects that populate our worlds. As we develop from babies to toddlers, to children, adolescents, and finally adults, we may break big ideas down into smaller pieces, in order to gain a better sense of the underpinnings that create the whole. We learn to explain our thinking through speech. But what about the body?

In the end, knowing and using the gesture types is a powerful way to move through the world, and get in touch with what you're trying to say (and what others are saying around you). Seen as a group, they form something of a user's manual for your physical communication. Through understanding and using the gesture types, people will better understand you and communicate back in a reciprocal way.

For many people, it's easier to be creative when they have defined parameters. Six gesture types is a great method to organize a massive amount of information in a digestible way. However, in truth, the study of gestures is pretty limitless. My goal with *Your Visual Connection* was to narrow the content in a way that helps you maximize what you're doing, and what you hope to do, within these studies. With this in mind, in the book's appendix section, you'll find a list of other tools and links to explore as you continue to move through the world with the help of the gesture types.

Integrating movement into any performance type can be a vital undertaking. Very few books and courses are talking about this, and most people remain unaware of how the gestures are constantly happening beneath everything we think, feel, and say. When we talk about making gestures, we tend to consider them to be things that happen, whether consciously or unconsciously, with our hands. My hope is that, with the help of *Your Visual Connection*, you've begun to see that there's much more to consider and know about the gesture types. It's interesting for me (and I hope for you as well) that in many ways, my journey toward completing this book started in an effort to answer a very similar question: "What should I do with my hands?"

Acknowledgments

Derek W.—Thank you for connecting me to an enlightening conversation every Friday morning.

Mary H.—Thank you for remembering my achievements. I wanted to let myself go and then you told my story again, with pride. It brought me back to life, and then you and Norma bought me breakfast.

To my Scribe team—Writing this book with y'all was a wonderful experience! Everyone was supportive, encouraging, and brave. I enjoyed collaborating with a smart, talented team that guided me through a well-structured journey. Thank you for facilitating this book.

To Dave Jarecki—We found our balance very early in the project and it gave me awesome courage. The way you "Yes, and…" taught me a great deal about collaboration in the

YOUR VISUAL CONNECTION

creative process. You're a game changer.

Alfredo Iriarte—Gracias por las fotos de la máscara neutral. Agradezco su ayuda.

Thomas Prattki—You teach the deepest roots that make world-class theatre.

Norman Taylor—For me, your week-long workshop(s) happened before class, in our random one-on-one morning conversations at a table in the coffee shop around the corner from the London studio. You talked of rhythm and then showed me the philosophy was about wonder. One week with you is worth two years in the best conservatories.

Gennadi Bogdanov—One of two people (recognized by Russia) to teach Meyerhold's method to the world - you bring more than your rich theatrical culture. We enacted your teachings in our morning commute to the studio, standing in the center of the bus that bravely surfed the sharp mountain curves outside of Perugia, Italy. You recalibrated my whole performance philosophy: thank you! (спасибо)

Sergei Ostrenko—Thank you for introducing me to the "whole world of theatre." Your lectures following those first workshops in Italy redefined my understanding of theatre.

Marianne K.—What you started in your movement class still resonates with me today.

Maura M.—I laugh a lot, like you did. I read a lot, like you did. Because of you, I am feeding songbirds and black crows. Thank you for your heritage, and the passport that goes along

ACKNOWLEDGMENTS

with it: this was unimaginable without you.

Kay S.—I was reborn at Bodywise! You ignited my love affair with movement! Thank you.

John M.—When I look back at your life, I see a lot of who I am today: sitting at a desk reading old books; joyful exuberance over a fresh and hot cup of coffee; and of course, your never-ending sense of play—to name a few. Thank you Dad for your constant encouragement, your unconditional love and support. I wish I could offer back half of what you give.

To my family—Hey y'all! Here's my book. I love you all very much.

Appendix

Online

Be sure to visit my website for more information, and to learn about classes, curriculum, training and more: *www.colum.info*.

Books on Acting, Performance, and Oration

Many books discuss the psychology of being an actor, but only a few give you a physical introduction of what to do, and help you go deeper into playing and developing your characters. Here is a list of books I return to again and again, and recommend to my students, as well as other actors and performance teachers:

Florence A. Fowle Adams, *Gesture and Pantomimic Action (Classic Reprint)*, Forgotten Books (2018), 233 pages, 1891

Angélique Arnaud, *Delsarte System of Oratory: Including the Complete Works of M. L'abbe Delaumosne and Mme. Angelique Arnaud (Pupils of Delsarte) With the Literary...Literally in Delsarte's Own Words, Without*, Sagwan Press (2018), 608 pages, 1893

Charles Aubert, *The Art of Pantomime*, Dover Publications (2003), 224 pages, 1927

Gilbert Austin, *Chironomia: Or, a Treatise on Rhetorical Delivery: Comprehending Many Precepts, Both Ancient and Modern, for the Proper Regulation of the Voice, the Countenance, and Gesture*, HardPress Publishing (2019), 654 pages, 1806

Carlo Blasis, *Notes upon dancing historical and practical by C. Blasis... Followed by a history of the Imperial and royal academy of dancing at Milan to which are added biographical notices of the Blasis family*, Generic (2019), 216 pages, 1847

E. M. Booth, *Outlines of the Delsarte System of Expression, Arranged for Use of Classes*, Wentworth Press (2016), 102 pages, 1890

John Bulwer, *Chirologia: Or the Natural Language of the Hand*, Literary Licensing, LLC (2014), 378 pages, 1644

Andrew Comstock, *A System of Elocution: With Special Reference to Gesture, to the Treatment of Stammering, and Defective Articulation*, Palala Press (2016), 400 pages, 1841

l'Abbe Delaumosne, *Pratique de l'art oratoire de Delsarte (French Edition)*, HardPress Publishing (2018), 1874

Anna Morgan, *An Hour with Delsarte (Classic Reprint): A Study of Expression*, Forgotten Books (2018), 165 pages, 1889

Antonio Morrocchesi, *Lezioni di declamazione e d'arte teatrale (Dialoghi) (Italian Edition)*, Gremese (1991), 366 pages, 1832

Simon Murray, *Jacques Lecoq (Routledge Performance Practitioners)*, Routledge (2017), 180 pages, 2017

APPENDIX

Genevieve Stebbins, *Delsarte system of dramatic expression*, Alpha Editions (2020), 296 pages, 1886

Edward Barrett Warman, *Gestures And Attitudes: An Exposition Of The Delsarte Philosophy Of Expression, Practical And Theoretical... One Hundred And Fifty-four Illustrations By Marion Morgan Reynolds*, Palala Press (2015), 438 pages, 1891

Maria Knebel, *L'analyse-action (French Edition)*, Actes Sud-Papiers.

Stella Adler, *The Art of Acting*, Applause (2000), Edition: First Edition, 288 pages, 2000

David Alberts, *The Expressive Body: Physical Characterization for the Actor*, Heinemann Drama (1997), 176 pages, 1997

Suzi Alderete, *re-Connect Your Dots, through the Anatomy Trains*, CreateSpace Independent Publishing Platform (2018), 142 pages, 2018

Andrea Morris, *The Science of On-Camera Acting*, Becoming Media (2014), 190 pages, 2014

Charles Aubert, *The Art of Pantomime*, Dover Publications (2003), 224 pages, 2003

Frances Babbage, *Augusto Boal (Routledge Performance Practitioners)*, Routledge (2004), 168 pages, 2004

Albert M. Bacon, *A Manual Of Gesture: Embracing A Complete System Of Notation, Together With The Principles Of Interpretation And Selections For Practice, By Albert M. Bacon. [rev. and enl.]*, Ulan Press (2012), 274 pages, 2012

Arthur Bartow, *Training of the American Actor*, Theatre Communications Group (2006), Edition: 1st Edition, 400 pages, 2006

Sandra Blakeslee, *The Body Has a Mind of Its Own: How Body Maps in Your Brain Help You Do (Almost) Everything Better*, Random House (2008), Edition: Reprint, 268 pages, 2008

Susana Bloch, *Alba Emoting: A Scientific Method for Emotional Induction*, CreateSpace Independent Publishing Platform (2017), 224 pages, 2017

Augusto Boal, *Theatre of the Oppressed*, Theatre Communications Group (1993), Edition: Tcg ed., 208 pages, 1993

Jan Bremmer, *A Cultural History of Gesture*, Cornell Univ Press (1992), Edition: 1st, 268 pages, 1992

Richard Brestoff, *The Great Acting Teachers and Their Methods (Career Development Series) (Career Development Book)*, Smith & Kraus (1996), Edition: 1st, 208 pages, 1996

Jane Drake Brody, *Acting, Archetype, and Neuroscience*, Routledge (2016), 172 pages, 2016

Dymphna Callery, *Through the Body: A Practical Guide to Physical Theatre (Theatre Arts (Routledge Paperback))*, Routledge (2002), 256 pages, 2002

Sharon Marie Carnicke, *Stanislavsky in Focus: An Acting Master for the Twenty-First Century (Routledge Theatre Classics)*, Routledge (2008), 272 pages, 2008

Franc Chamberlain, *Jacques Lecoq and the British Theatre (Contemporary Theatre Studies)*, Routledge (2002), 140 pages, 2002

Michael Chekhov, *To the Actor: On the Technique of Acting*, Martino Fine Books (2014), Edition: Illustrated, 220 pages, 2014

Nicholas Dromgoole, *Performance, Style and Gesture in Western Theatre*, Oberon Books (2008), 320 pages, 2008

Sears A. Eldredge, *Mask Improvisation for Actor Training and Performance: The Compelling Image*, Northwestern University Press (1996), Edition: 1, 208 pages, 1996

Johann Jakob Engle, *Practical Illustrations of Rhetorical Gesture and Action*, Wentworth Press (2016), 2016

William Esper, *The Actor's Art and Craft: William Esper Teaches the Meisner Technique*, Anchor (2008), Edition: 1, 304 pages, 2008

William Esper, *The Actor's Guide to Creating a Character: William Esper Teaches the Meisner Technique*, Anchor (2014), 304 pages, 2014

APPENDIX

Mark Evans, *Jacques Copeau (Routledge Performance Practitioners)*, Routledge (2006), 192 pages, 2006

Mark Evans, *Movement Training for the Modern Actor (Routledge Advances in Theatre and Performance Studies)*, Routledge (2010), 224 pages, 2010

Antonio Fava, *The Comic Mask in the Commedia dell'Arte: Actor Training, Improvisation, and the Poetics of Survival*, Northwestern University Press (2007), Edition: 1, 262 pages, 2007

Susan Goldin-Meadow, *Hearing Gesture: How Our Hands Help Us Think*, Belknap Press: An Imprint of Harvard University Press (2005), Edition: New Ed, 304 pages, 2005

Mel Gordon, *The Stanislavsky Technique: Russia: A Workbook for Actors (Applause Acting Series)*, Applause (2000), Edition: 1st, 272 pages, 2000

Uta Hagen, *A Challenge for The Actor*, Charles Scribner's Sons (1991), Edition: 1st, 336 pages, 1991

Uta Hagen, *Respect for Acting*, Wiley (2008), Edition: 2nd Edition, 240 pages, 2008

Halpern, *Truth in Comedy: The Manual of Improvisation*, Christian Publishers LLC (1994), Edition: Illustrated, 150 pages, 1994

John Harrop, *Acting with Style, 3rd Edition*, Allyn and Bacon (1999), Edition: 3rd, 352 pages, 1999

Alan E. Hicks, *Singer and Actor: Acting Technique and the Operatic Performer (Amadeus)*, Amadeus (2011), 196 pages, 2011

Will Hines, *How to Be the Greatest Improviser on Earth*, Pretty Great Publishing (2016), 232 pages, 2016

Alison Hodge, *Twentieth-Century Actor Training*, Routledge (1999), 272 pages,1999

Thomas James, *A Director's Guide to Stanislavsky's Active Analysis: Including the Formative Essay on Active Analysis by Maria Knebel*, Methuen Drama (2016), 192 pages, 2016

Keith Johnstone, *Impro (Performance Books): Improvisation and the Theatre (Performance Books)*, Methuen Drama (2007), Edition: 1st, 208 pages, 2007

Claude Kipnis, *The mime book (An Umbrella book)*, Harper & Row (1974), Edition: 1st, 226 pages, 1974

Howard Kissel, *Stella Adler: The Art of Acting*, Echo Point Books & Media, LLC (2022), 2022

Alma Law, *Meyerhold, Eisenstein and Biomechanics: Actor Training in Revolutionary Russia*, McFarland & Co (2012), Edition: Illustrated, 294 pages, 2012

Thomas Leabhart, *Etienne Decroux (Routledge Performance Practitioners)*, Routledge (2018), 164 pages, 2018

Jacques Lecoq, *The Moving Body (Le Corps Poétique): Teaching creative theatre (Theatre Makers)*, Methuen Drama (2020), Edition: 3, 232 pages, 2020

Jacques Lecoq, *Theatre of Movement and Gesture*, Routledge (2006), 184 pages, 2006

Marion Lowell, *Harmonic Gymnastics and Pantomimic Expression*, Andesite Press (2017), 368 pages, 2017

Michael Lugering, *The Expressive Actor: Integrated Voice, Movement, and Acting Training*, Heinemann Drama (2007), 240 pages, 2007

David Mamet, *True and False: Heresy and Common Sense for the Actor*, Pantheon Books (1997), Edition: 1st, 127 pages, 1997

Lorna Marshall, *An Actor's Tricks (Performance Books)*, Methuen Drama (2013), Edition: 1, 114 pages, 2013

Bella Merlin, *Beyond Stanislavsky: The Psycho-Physical Approach to Actor Training*, Routledge (2001), 276 pages, 2001

Bella Merlin, *The Complete Stanislavsky Toolkit*, Quite Specific Media Group Ltd (2007), Edition: 1st, 352 pages, 2007

Bruce Miller, *The Actor as Storyteller: An Introduction to Acting*, Limelight (2012), Edition: 2nd ed., 344 pages, 2012

APPENDIX

Sonia Moore, *The Stanislavski System: The Professional Training of an Actor; Second Revised Edition (Penguin Handbooks)*, Penguin Books (1984), Edition: 2nd Revised ed., 112 pages, 1984

Nick Moseley, *Actioning—and How to Do It*, Nick Hern Books (2017), 160 pages, 2017

A. M. Nagler, *A Source Book in Theatrical History: Twenty-five centuries of stage history in more than 300 basic documents and other primary material*, Dover Publications (1959), Edition: Annotated, 640 pages, 1959

Yoshi Oida, *The Invisible Actor (Bloomsbury Revelations)*, Bloomsbury Academic (2020), Edition: Reprint, 128 pages, 2020

Adrian Pecknold, *Mime: The Step Beyond Words : For the Actors of Dance and Drama*, NC Press Limited (1989), Edition: Revised Edition, 152 pages, 1989

Litz Pisk, *The Actor and His Body (Performance Books)*, Methuen Drama (2006), 96 pages, 2006

Jonathan Pitches, *Vsevolod Meyerhold (Routledge Performance Practitioners)*, Routledge (2003), 176 pages, 2003

Nicole Potter, *Movement for Actors*, Allworth Press (2002), Edition: 1st, 288 pages, 2002

Mark Rafael, *Telling Stories: The Grand Unifying Theory of Acting Techniques (Career Development Series)*, Smith & Kraus (2008), 208 pages, 2008

Thomas Richards, *At Work with Grotowski on Physical Actions*, Routledge (1995), 152 pages, 1995

Bari Rolfe, *Actions Speak Louder: A Workbook for Actors*, Personabooks (1992), 68 pages, 1992

Bari Rolfe, *Mimes on Miming: Writings on Art of Music*, Panjandrum (1979), Edition: First Printing - Stated, 1979

James Roose-Evans, *Experimental Theatre: From Stanislavsky to Peter Brook*, Universe Pub (1984), Edition: 3, 210 pages, 1984

Joanna Rotté, *Acting with Adler (Limelight)*, Limelight (2004), Edition: 1st Limelight ed, 194 pages, 2000

John Rudlin, *Commedia Dell'Arte: An Actor's Handbook*, Routledge (1994), 296 pages, 1994

Jean Sabatine, *Movement Training for the Stage and Screen: The Organic Connection Between Mind, Spirit, and Body*, Backstage Books (1995), 239 pages, 1995

Athene Seyler, *The Craft of Comedy*, Routledge (2013), 176 pages, 2013

Ted Shawn, *Every Little Movement: A Book About Delsarte*, Dance Horizons (2016), Edition: 1, 154 pages, 2016

Michael Shurtleff, *Audition*, Bantam (1979), Edition: Reissue, 288 pages, 1978

E. Simon, *Masking Unmasked: Four Approaches to Basic Acting*, Palgrave Macmillan (2004), Edition: 1st, 205 pages, 2004

Fay Simpson, *The Lucid Body: A Guide for the Physical Actor*, Allworth (2008), Edition: 1, 224 pages, 2008

Constantin Stanislavski, *An Actor Prepares*, Echo Point Books & Media, LLC (2020), 2020

Constantin Stanislavski, *Building A Character*, Routledge (1989), 207 pages, 1989

Constantin Stanislavski, *Creating A Role*, Theatre Arts Books (1961), 292 pages, 1961

Vasily Osipovich Toporkov, *Stanislavski in Rehearsal (Theatre Arts Book)*, Routledge (2004), 184 pages, 2004

Stephen Wangh, *An Acrobat of the Heart: A Physical Approach to Acting Inspired by the Work of Jerzy Grotowski*, Vintage (2000), Edition: 1st, 384 pages, 2000

Toby Wilsher, *The Mask Handbook: A Practical Guide*, Routledge (2006), 200 pages, 2006

APPENDIX

Books on Business, Psychology, and Communication Studies

The following books offer new ways to explore the gestures that go beyond performance:

Nancy Armstrong, *Field Guide to Gestures: How to Identify and Interpret Virtually Every Gesture Known to Man*, Quirk Books (2015), 320 pages, 2015
Charles Francis Atkinson, *Art and Artist: Creative Urge and Personality Development*, W. W. Norton & Company (1989), 534 pages, 1989
Michael Argyle, *Bodily Communication*, Routledge (2010), 380 pages, 2010
Geoffrey Beattie, *Visible Thought: The New Psychology of Body Language*, Routledge (2004), 216 pages, 2003
Eric Berne, *Games People Play: The Basic Handbook of Transactional Analysis*, Ballantine Books (1996), 216 pages, 1996
Paul Ekman Ph.D., *Emotions Revealed, Second Edition: Recognizing Faces and Feelings to Improve Communication and Emotional Life*, Holt Paperbacks (2007), Edition: 2nd, 320 pages, 2007
Mircea Eliade, *The Forge and the Crucible: The Origins and Structure of Alchemy*, University of Chicago Press (1979), Edition: Second, 238 pages, 1979
Gordon Emmerson, *Ego State Therapy*, Crown House Publishing (2007), 232 pages, 2007
Erving Goffman, *The Presentation of Self in Everyday Life*, Bantam Doubleday Dell Publishing Group (1959), Edition: later Printing, 255 pages, 1959
Ellen Goldman, *As Others See Us: Body Movement and the Art of Successful Communication*, Routledge (2003), 228 pages, 2003

John Graham, *Outdoor Leadership: Technique, Common Sense, & Self-Confidence*, Mountaineers Books (1997), Edition: 1, 176 pages, 1997

Peggy Hackney, *Making Connections: Total Body Integration Through Bartenieff Fundamentals*, Routledge (2000), 272 pages, 2000

Mark Johnson, *The Body in the Mind: The Bodily Basis of Meaning, Imagination, and Reason*, University of Chicago Press (1990), Edition: 1, 272 pages, 1990

Rick Kemp, *Embodied Acting: What Neuroscience Tells Us About Performance*, Routledge (2012), 256 pages, 2012

George Lakoff & Mark Johnson, *Metaphors We Live By*, University of Chicago Press (2003), Edition: 1st, 242 pages, 2003

George Lakoff & Mark Johnson, *Philosophy In the Flesh: The Embodied Mind and Its Challenge To Western Thought*, Basic Books (1999), Edition: First Edition, 640 pages, 1999

David Matsumoto, *Nonverbal Communication: Science and Applications*, SAGE Publications, Inc (2012), Edition: 1, 336 pages, 2012

David McNeill, *Gesture and Thought*, University Of Chicago Press (2005), 328 pages, 2005

David McNeill, *Hand and Mind: What Gestures Reveal about Thought*, University of Chicago Press (1996), Edition: New edition, 423 pages, 1996

Albert Mehrabian, *Silent Messages: Implicit Communication of Emotions and Attitudes*, Wadsworth Pub Co (1980), Edition: 2nd, 196 pages, 1980

Emily Post, *Emily Post's Etiquette*, HarperCollins (1984), Edition: 14th/Index, 1018 pages, 1984

Author Bio

Colum Parke Morgan, an international performance coach, actor, and teacher, specializes in American and European performance methods, including masks and biomechanics. A certified acting teacher, Colum earned his BFA in Music & Theatre from University of Kansas-Lawrence, and his MFA in Acting from University of Texas-Austin.

Well-versed in European theatre traditions, Colum previously studied in small group and private workshop settings with Norman Taylor (Lecoq training), Gennadi Bogdanov (Meyerhold's Biomechanics), Theatre de l'Ange Fou (Decroux's Corporeal Mime), Larry Silverberg (Meisner training), Robin Carr (Lessac Voice training), Sergei Ostrenko (Russian GITIS training), and Thomas Prattki (IMPP).

A seasoned performer and professional actor, Colum has worked and performed in a range of styles, including improvisation, children's theatre, melodrama, vaudeville, musicals, classical and devised theatre. He has appeared and performed in film and TV, on radio, and onstage in many settings throughout parts of the U.S., Europe, Pacific Islands, Central America, North Africa and elsewhere.

Colum possesses TEFL certification (Teaching English as a Foreign Language), and has taught in Paris, Berlin, and San Francisco. His career as a performance teacher and mentor began in 2012, and continues to span a number of geographies, cultures, and settings. His stops include launching the Actor's Gym series of acting classes at Salles Saint Roch (Paris) and facilitating private coaching sessions for non-actors. Today, his work frequently finds him leading corporate and small business workshops and lessons, where he guides individuals toward integrating movement into their everyday practice.

Your Visual Connection is his first book. You can learn more about his work, career, and teaching, and access additional resources online at *www.colum.info*.

www.ingramcontent.com/pod-product-compliance
Lightning Source LLC
Chambersburg PA
CBHW060521080526
44586CB00012B/564